FRIENDLY FIRE

FRIENDLY FIRE

The Near-Death of the
TRANSATLANTIC ALLIANCE

ELIZABETH POND

EUROPEAN UNION STUDIES ASSOCIATION
Pittsburgh, Pennsylvania

BROOKINGS INSTITUTION PRESS
Washington, D.C.

Friendly Fire may be ordered from:
Brookings Institution Press
1775 Massachusetts Avenue, N.W.,
Washington, D.C. 20036
Tel. 1-800/275-1447 or 202/797-6258
Fax: 202/797-2960
www.brookings.edu

Library of Congress Cataloging-in-Publication data

Pond, Elizabeth.
Friendly fire : the near-death of the transatlantic alliance /
Elizabeth Pond.
p. cm.
Includes bibliographical references and index.
ISBN 0-8157-7153-3 (pbk. : alk. paper)
1. United States—Military relations—Europe. 2. Europe—Military
relations—United States. 3. United States—Foreign relations—Europe.
4. Europe—Foreign relations—United States. 5. United States—
Military policy. 6. United States—Foreign relations—2001–
7. World politics—1995–2005. I. Title.

UA23.P549 2003
327.7304—dc22   2003019910

9 8 7 6 5 4 3 2 1
The paper used in this publication meets minimum requirements of the American
National Standard for Information Sciences—Permanence of Paper for Printed Library
Materials: ANSI Z39.48-1992.

Typeset in Minion

Composition by OSP, Arlington, Virginia

Printed by R. R. Donnelley, Harrisonburg, Virginia

CONTENTS

FOREWORD

THIS IS THE FIFTH monograph in the European Union Studies Association's U.S.-EU Relations Project series, and it comes at a time of continuing crisis. Elizabeth Pond began this book during the buildup to the war in Iraq. She presented the first draft at a roundtable at the Center for Strategic and International Studies in Washington, D.C., on January 24, 2003, a moment when relations between the United States and France and Germany had taken a particularly bad turn. Around the table were discussants from all of the major European embassies, as well as from the U.S. Departments of State and Defense, other government agencies, academe, and think tanks. On the basis of the rich and revealing discussion at this meeting, Pond reworked her material and presented it at the EUSA Eighth Biennial International Conference in Nashville, which took place at the height of the war, in March 2003. The finished volume appears at a time when transatlantic relations are clearly in need of reconstruction. Therefore, the importance of this work has grown during the period between its conception and its publication.

Elizabeth Pond is ideally placed as an analyst of transatlantic relations. An American who has lived for many years in Europe, she has been a journalist, a teacher, and a scholar. Both she and EUSA owe a considerable debt to those who have made EUSA's fifth U.S.-EU Relations Project possible. The idea originated with discussions among my colleagues on the 2001–03 EUSA Executive Committee: Karen Alter, Jeffrey Anderson, George Bermann, Donald Hancock, Mark Pollack, and George Ross. Simon Serfaty, director of the Europe Program, Center for Strategic and

International Studies, generously hosted the Washington, D.C., workshop. The German Marshall Fund of the United States gave important financial support for this workshop and the roundtable at the EUSA conference in Nashville. The membership of the European Union Studies Association helped underwrite the publication of the monograph through their membership dues, and they receive a complimentary copy as a benefit of membership. Robert Faherty, director of Brookings Institution Press, deserves credit for his continued interest in the U.S.-EU Relations Project monographs. Finally, the project would not have been possible without the hands-on direction of Valerie Staats, executive director of EUSA.

MARTIN A. SCHAIN
Chair, European Union Studies Association, 2001–03

PREFACE

THIS BOOK IS A second draft of the bizarre history of the decay and threatened dissolution of the West in 2002–03. At this early date it does not aspire to completeness. It does, however, aspire to fairness in portraying the most important of the cumulative brawls that led to the near-death of the transatlantic alliance in 2002–03. Given the angry polemics that accompanied each twist and turn, this is no modest goal. There is as yet no generally agreed basic narrative of precisely what happened, how, and why. Conflicting virtual realities abound.

The study was commissioned by the European Union Studies Association to examine post–9/11 security issues in the transatlantic community that the world's sole superpower invented half a century ago. It assumes that the process we are witnessing today is a double adjustment: to the new threats of terrorism and proliferation of weapons of mass destruction on the one hand, and to the Pax Americana of a polity wielding more absolute power than any since ancient Rome on the other hand. It assumes further that relations in the transatlantic community that was formed after 1945 were in greater crisis in 2003 than ever before. This last thesis is far less contested today than when I, among others, first propounded it in the spring of 2002. By early 2003 no less a judge than master diplomat Henry Kissinger, relativizing all the past fights over missile deployments, chicken exports, and even France's imperious withdrawal from NATO's military command in the mid-1960s, ranked the transatlantic estrangement as the worst in a half century.[1] Secretary of State Colin Powell seconded the judgment in speaking of the alliance as breaking up.

The indexes of the gravity of this crisis were the broad spectrum of mutually reinforcing disputes, the accompanying vitriol, and, of course, the divergence in self-identification on the two sides of the Atlantic.

In the past, however heated the confrontations, transatlantic quarrels tended to be over single issues, or at most two or three questions at a time, not over a whole range of topics that obstructed conciliation on any one of them and maximized ill will. By 2003 the list of differences was long—not only the Iraq war, the monopoly on agenda setting by the world's hyperpower, the U.S. demand for obedience rather than counsel from its allies, rivalry for the hearts and minds of new central European entrants to the North Atlantic Treaty Organization and the European Union, the proper role of the United Nations and international law, and treatment of prisoners from Afghanistan in the legal limbo of the American base at Guantanamo Bay in Cuba, but also development of tactical nuclear weapons, the International Criminal Court, the Kyoto Protocol on curbing greenhouse gases, the series of arms treaties on land mines, nuclear test bans, and enforcement of bans on chemical and biological weapons, along with genetically modified foods, privacy, and the like. Together, these controversies exacerbated one another. Moreover, they are further reinforced by long-standing mutual disapproval of domestic social choices made on the other side of the Atlantic. The American political class, with some resonance in the public, was critical of what it saw as excessive social welfare, high labor costs that discourage entrepreneurs from creating jobs, and other rigidities in Europe's sluggish economies. Conversely, many in the continental European political class were appalled by what they regard as callousness toward life's unfortunates in the United States—along with excessive violence, casual access to guns, the world's highest per capita prison population, and a racially biased death sentence.

The second measure of transatlantic tension was the bad temper, especially in the widespread disdain for Europe in official Washington. "Anti-Europeanism," as brought to public attention especially by Timothy Garton Ash,[2] was not just a clever intellectual foil to anti-Americanism. Nor was it a minor phenomenon, given its effect on policy. At the benign end, it was simply a writing off of Europe, the conclusion that Europe had become irrelevant and did not matter any more. By early 2002, in the view of the neoconservatives who were increasingly giving the tone to the

Bush administration, America's important allies were the Latin Americans, or even the Russians.[3] Europe was no longer at the heart of international politics as it had been during the cold war. Europeans were unimportant. They had become the victims of their own success in establishing on their continent, finally, a liberal peace. Europe no longer posed the danger of war (except in the Balkans, and even this region was gradually being tamed) and was therefore uninteresting for a superpower with global responsibilities. If Europeans were too cowardly to join America's defense of the West, they could be ignored.

In a more corrosive form, such indifference shaded over into a deep contempt in Washington for what was viewed as European military weakness and political softness. This attitude was especially pronounced among those civilian Pentagon officials who have led the American revolution in foreign policy, but it was by no means confined to them. The outrage boiled up as well in numerous American Europeanists who speak foreign languages, have lived in Europe for years, and bristle at any European pretension to play the wise Greeks to America's muscle-bound Romans.

Two anecdotes give the flavor. One senior German newspaper editor with a stellar pro-American track record interviewed National Security Council adviser Condoleezza Rice in early 2002. As he was being escorted out of the office by someone he knew from the latter's earlier stays in Europe, he had his ears pinned back by the staff member's passionate, out-of-the-blue warning: Don't you Europeans tell us what to do! And don't think you're smarter than we are, because you aren't![4]

Similarly, when the ebullient and equally pro-American Ludger Kühnhardt, director of the Bonn Center for the Study of European Integration, visited a State Department section chief in the summer of 2002, he was greeted at the door with a blast about what the Europeans were doing wrong, what a waste of time the regular U.S.-European summits were, and what a terrible job various European ambassadors were doing in Washington. The only possible response, he related later, was to ask if he might be allowed to sit down anyway.

Third, what journalists would call the "story line" has diverged sharply on the two sides of the Atlantic, within the lifetime of today's leaders. The dichotomy goes well beyond what Robert Kagan famously identified as the gap between American power and European weakness, though this lacuna is a major manifestation of the divergence. For half a century we have proclaimed that the United States and Europe share the same values, and this is certainly true in the fundamental sense of democracy, rule of law, market economy, and civil society. What seems to be happening now, though, is that in many cases our particular social and political embodiments of these precepts are themselves being elevated to the level of fundamental values. As the German Foreign Ministry coordinator for German-American cooperation, Karsten Voigt, often notes, the end of the cold war and the Soviet threat has relaxed our earlier compulsion to tolerate differences in our secondary values in view of our overriding common interest in the survival of our first-rank values.[5] We now think we have the luxury of abandoning this tolerance. And the quarrels that then bubble up are particularly intractable because one side or both see these as matters of conscience—especially in such issues as the death penalty, abortion, genetically modified foods, and the social net. Daniel Hamilton, director of the Center for Transatlantic Relations at the Paul H. Nitze School of Advanced International Studies at Johns Hopkins University, adds that it is precisely because our societies have become so closely knit in a "quasi domestic" relationship that disputes penetrate far beyond the shallow level of the old trade wars and "affect such fundamental domestic issues as the ways Americans and Europeans are taxed, how our societies are governed, or how our economies are regulated."[6]

Under these circumstances, while it touches on structural analysis, this book concentrates more on the context, texture, and proximate dynamics at each point. It necessarily pays attention to the unusually high incidence of personal pique and tactical maneuver that have repeatedly erupted into belligerence and defied all the logic of the interdependent $2.5 trillion transatlantic economy.[7] It notes that any traditional realist glancing at the figures would instantly conclude that the two shores of the Atlantic are condemned to cooperate, in their own mutual interest. Europeans hold two-thirds of all foreign assets in the United States, generate half of all corporate America's overseas profits, create almost twelve million high-paying jobs in the United States, and go far toward offsetting America's $1.4 billion daily current account deficits. The transatlantic economies are huge, generating two-thirds of world product and half of global trade. Americans and Europeans invest more in each other's businesses than they do in all the rest of the world, with European investment in the United States helpfully topping reciprocal investment from the world's largest debtor by some 25 percent. So intertwined have transatlantic companies become, especially in the past decade, that it is often impossible to tell if firms are actually "American" or "European."[8] U.S. Trade Representative Robert Zoellick cited comparable statistics to help relaunch the Doha trade round shortly after 9/11. Reversing the fear at the end of the cold war that all the banana and steel wars would split the United States and Europe once the discipline of the Soviet threat vanished, he held out the obverse hope that our economic need for each other could help salve political wounds in the transatlantic relationship. His appeal did help win congressional support for the new talks to lower trade barriers, though it had no broader impact.

As with my previous books, this one too assumes that there is (still) a transatlantic continuum that constitutes a common political home for Americans and Europeans alike. And as with my previous books, it takes Berlin as a prism through which to understand developments in Europe. To be sure, Germany was not the main protagonist in the drama. American-French animosity quickly surpassed the American-German feud in virulence, and Chancellor Gerhard Schröder, under President George W. Bush's ostracism of him after the German election in September 2002, essentially abdicated from foreign policy altogether for months. Nonetheless, Germany is still the largest nation on the continent, a third more populous than any of the other big states of France, Britain, Italy, Spain, and Poland; it is the European Union's economic pacesetter, the third richest country in the world, and the model for European Monetary Union; until 2003 it typically served the important function of allaying reciprocal French and American suspicions; and Germans, as the most Americanized of any Europeans (far more so than the English), hold up a special mirror to the United States.

Moreover, as the cold war ended, the Germans were the only Europeans to formulate a *gesamtkonzept,* or coherent road map of where Europe should be heading in the rare decade of international flux that would follow and to press for both "widening" and "deepening" of the European Union. Chancellor Helmut Kohl set the agenda for the next stage of the "ever closer union" envisaged in the 1957 Treaty of Rome. His determination to embed his countrymen in a progressively integrating Europe that would share its precious security and prosperity with the new democracies to the east finally solved the old "German question" of restless Teutons, averted the turbulence of previous German unification and ascents in 1870, 1914, and 1939—and proved that Europe's supranational cooperation was no freak by-product of the Soviet threat, but a permanent rejection of a two-millennium history of bloodshed. For all of these reasons—and not just because the traditional German concept of adult European partnership with the American hyperpower suggests a middle way between French president Jacques Chirac's rebellion against the United States and British prime minister Tony Blair's reverence for it—Berlin remains a key player in the ongoing story.

In this study I devote one chapter each to the shock of 9/11; the emerging transatlantic misgivings in early 2002; the German-American-French strains over the impending war from August 2002 to the opening shots on March 19, 2003; and the aftermath of the Iraq war as American disillusionment set in.

I would like to thank the EUSA for provoking me to write this study; the German Marshall Fund of the United States for providing some enabling funds; commenters on earlier drafts of this book at the American Institute for Contemporary German Studies in October 2002, at the Center for Strategic and International Studies in January 2003, and at the EUSA biennial conference in March 2003; the commenters on my penultimate draft, David Schoenbaum, Elisabeth Wendt, and anonymous American and German reviewers; and my editor, Deborah M. Styles. I would also like to thank everyone I interviewed (listed at the back of the book), as well as other interlocutors in more informal conversations, for the wealth of insights and concerns they shared with me. If I have rarely credited the latter with their specific contributions, discretion is the reason for this silence. The views expressed here, the surviving clichés, and, of course, any mistakes are mine alone.

Berlin, July 21, 2003

FRIENDLY FIRE

CHAPTER ONE

PAX AMERICANA

The Shock of 9/11

IN THE BEGINNING were Paul Wolfowitz, Robert Kagan, and their soul mates. Or so it seemed, once the U.S. deputy secretary of defense announced the death of permanent coalitions like the North Atlantic Treaty Organization (NATO) at the high-powered Munich Security Conference in February 2002 and the relatively unknown policy wonk published his essay on "Power and Weakness" a few months later and captivated the chattering classes.[1]

U.S. Defense Secretary Donald Rumsfeld, who skipped the previously mandatory conference to pursue the al Qaeda terrorists who had been identified as the 9/11 perpetrators, had already declared that from now on the mission would determine the coalition, and not vice versa. The implications had not sunk in, however; in late 2002 and early 2003 European reproaches about the American failure to accept the major help NATO had offered right after 9/11 tended to treat this U.S. lapse as an oversight that could perhaps be corrected if only the Americans and Europeans reasoned together.[2] In Munich, however, Wolfowitz repeated Rumsfeld's phrase and made it brutally clear that the snub to NATO was intentional, despite the alliance's unprecedented invocation of Article 5 of its founding treaty in branding the 9/11 attack on America an attack on all NATO members.[3] He brushed aside European worries about Bush's ignoring of the Europeans in the State of the Union address a few days earlier and the president's depiction of Iraq, Iran, and North Korea as an "axis of evil."[4] He did not bother to address the 'other administration actions that had just aroused European apprehension: the unilateral abrogation in December of the three-decade-old Anti-Ballistic Missile Treaty in order to build an anti-ballistic missile shield for the United States—and the concurrent agreement with Russia on cuts in nuclear warheads, which, for the first time in such treaties, would be not destroyed but simply stored, revocably. He gave no hint of the secret Defense Department policy review that was considering use of nuclear weapons against the three "axis" states.[5] Nor did he hint at the secret "Team B" intelligence unit that he, Rumsfeld, and Undersecretary of Defense for Policy Douglas Feith had set up in the Pentagon in October to pressure the regular intelligence agencies into more hawkish evaluations of Iraqi and other threats.[6] And if Wolfowitz had any compunction, as a mere deputy secretary, about lecturing a room full of European defense ministers and other movers and shakers, he betrayed no sign of it. Nor did the visiting American senators and congressmen leave any doubt that they had come to judge the European parliamentarians and governments represented in Munich—and were finding them wanting.

Indeed, far from according the Europeans any credit for the spontaneous alliance solidarity after 9/11, Wolfowitz went on the offensive in Munich, berating the continental Europeans for lagging far behind America in the technological revolution in military affairs (RMA), fielding inefficient armed forces, and not being able to fight alongside the United States. In future operations Washington would pick and choose its assistance from NATO and various bilateral forces inside and outside NATO. This was the "toolbox" approach to the alliance, in the term that would come into vogue. NATO allies would have no privileged position and would certainly not be allowed to veto targets or tactics, as the United States said they had done in the Kosovo war. Moreover, the sly Europeans were warned not to provoke the United States by trying to extract influence over Washington's decisions as a price for any military contributions they might offer and America might accept.

As the repercussions from the Munich conference were still reverberating, Kagan acknowledged that Rumsfeld and Wolfowitz might not always be the administration's "most effective salesmen on this issue. Their evident disdain for the NATO allies, and for world opinion in general, has unnecessarily hurt Bush's cause abroad."[7]

In his essay Kagan was somewhat more tactful, and more cerebral, but he delivered the same message about America's ordained role in holding the barbarians far from the gates in the new world disorder after 9/11 and about the gratitude and loyalty others owed the United States for this service.

As British diplomat Robert Cooper subsequently noted, there are gifted authors who, with exquisite timing, capture a partial truth at a point when their aperçu seizes the public imagination.[8] Yale's Paul Kennedy had done so at a rare moment of American self-doubt and pessimism in the 1980s, when he popularized the notion of "imperial overstretch"[9]—and was immediately rebutted by Harvard's Joseph Nye in his exploration of America's extraordinary "soft power,"[10] as well as by America's irrational financial exuberance in the 1990s and political exuberance in the twenty-first century. Francis Fukuyama had pulled off the feat with his essay "The End of History" as the Soviet Union collapsed and the cold war dissipated.[11] Kagan now found comparable resonance as wounded Americans groped to make sense of their new universe after 9/11.

Simply put, his thesis was that the benevolent American hegemon was and should be unilaterally assertive around the globe, because its singular power let it bestride the world like a colossus. Americans were tough Hobbesians; Europeans were timid Kantian appeasers. Americans were from Mars; Europeans were from Venus. The Europeans, armed with no more than a knife, shunned confrontation with the bear in the forest; Americans, sensibly armed with a gun, aggressively sought confrontation to eliminate the ursine threat. Inhabitants of the eastern shores of the Atlantic Ocean, though dependent on American protection, sought to block the exercise of American might only because they themselves lacked power. So different have the two partners become, Kagan concluded, that it is time "to stop pretending that Europeans and Americans share a common view of the world, or even that they occupy the same world."[12]

Suddenly there was a Big Idea to end the floundering for a new paradigm for post-Soviet foreign policy. America's war on terrorism, declared hours after the Twin Towers collapse, now had a coherent intellectual underpinning. Antiterrorism, holding open a policy option of preventive war (or "preemptive" war, as it would come to be labeled inaccurately),[13] would be the new organizing principle. The United States should defend itself by combating terrorism around the globe—and take prudent measures to ensure that no other power could ever rise to challenge its supremacy. For neoconservatives this approach was plain common sense.[14] For many other post–9/11 readers, by contrast, Kagan's parsimonious explanation was a revelation. Within weeks his essay was a mandatory reference in every public debate.

There was no lack of alternative, if less popular, frameworks of analysis. Purists disputed Kagan's interpretation of Immanuel Kant, if not necessarily the 1990s' metamorphosis of Kant's eighteenth-century theory of a liberal peace into a twentieth-century theory of peace between democracies.[15] Various other critics noted that even if the British, for the sake of argument, were classified as honorary Americans rather than Europeans, this still left the very European French exhibiting quite martial characteristics. They recalled too British prime minister Tony Blair's desperate campaign—against Washington's stiff resistance—to get the United States to put boots on the ground in the Kosovo war in 1999. (To this Kagan supporters retorted that wars for national interest, and not wars for feel-good humanitarian causes, were the issue; that President Bill Clinton was hardly the kind of red-blooded American they were extolling; and that, anyway, when they said "Europeans," this might best be understood as a code word for their real enemies, the Democrats.)

More analytically, Karl Kaiser, outgoing director of studies at the German Council on Foreign Relations, sees the basic tension of our era not as a contradiction between American power and European weakness, but rather as one between American dominance and the inherent interdependence of globalization.[16] Nye, continuing his exploration of soft power, notes that while Kagan's revered national military might may be the crucial determinant on the first dimension of power, more diffuse transnational economic power reigns on the second dimension—and even superwarriors are of limited use against terrorists on the third dimension of nonstate actors with access to fantastic destructive power in a globalized world.[17] Javier Solana, the European Union's High Representative for Common Foreign and Security Policy, picks up the same point in stating, "Getting others to want what you want can be much more efficient in getting others to do what you want"—and pleading for a marriage of Mars and Venus that could lead to the birth, as in the original myth, of the beautiful goddess Harmonia.[18]

Simon Serfaty, veteran director of the Europe Project at the Center for Strategic and International Studies, finds that a "more relevant" dichotomy than Kagan's power/weakness is power/order.[19] Philip Gordon, director of the Center on the United States and France at the Brookings Institution, also contests Kagan's assumptions, arguing that "structure is not destiny" and the real issue is instead players' deliberate choices of "strategic culture." Gordon further protests against Kagan's conclusion "that the advent of the most socially conservative and internationally unilateralist administration in Washington in more than twenty years—after the most closely contested election in history—represents some fundamental shift in 'American' culture or values."[20]

Robert Cooper and Harvard's J. H. H. Weiler also part company with Kagan in viewing the differential transatlantic evolutions of the past half century through a far more pro-European lens. Cooper, now chief adviser to High Representative Javier Solana, spends much of his time prodding EU members to take the new threats more seriously and to boost their defenses, in an effort that Kagan would approve. Yet he also appreciates Europe's new art of cooperation—as measured most dramatically, he notes, in the routine interference by EU members in one another's internal affairs—which has rendered obsolete the continent's warring habits of earlier millennia.[21] Notably, years before September 11, 2001, he foreshadowed the problems that would confront the kind of postmodern, anti-war European states when their civilized nonviolence collided with the "premodern" stratum of often warring and/or failing states (like Afghanistan), or even "modern" nationalist states (like China and the United States). In such cases double standards, including even tolerance for preemptive military action against premodern tyrants, might be needed, he suggested.

Weiler addresses one aspect of Cooper's institutionalized outside interference in domestic affairs in focusing on an element of Europe's post–World War II consensus system that baffles most Americans—the willingness of independent states to "pool" their sovereignty in the conviction that each is too small to solve environmental, financial, and other problems in a globalized world, and that they therefore gain more control over their fate when they work together. Never, in the American vocabulary, would the positive verb "pool" replace the negative concept of "surrendering" sovereignty to a supranational entity. Weiler began his studies by working the puzzle of why powerful governments have for decades voluntarily accepted the authority of a European Court of Justice with no enforcement arm of its own—even to the point of letting national laws be overruled.[22] He ended by applying the logic of Albert O. Hirschman's protean concept of voice and exit to the post–World War II evolution of European integration. Weiler observed that the six countries that signed the 1957 Treaty of Rome initially thought their pact was revocable and that whenever the cost-benefit balance turned unfavorable, they could leave the European Community. What they and the other nations that more than doubled EU membership by the mid-1990s found out again and again, however, was that once they had begun profiting from the expanded possibilities that the European Community/European Union (EC/EU) conferred, the costs of "exit" were always too high, whatever the frustrations. Each time they rediscovered this verity, they returned to intramural negotiations with renewed vigor, demanding the alternative of enlarging their own voice within the evolving system and thus deepening European integration.[23]

9/11 and the Neoconservatives

In the first decade after the end of the cold war the contrasting European and American political styles that had existed since the end of World War II did not matter very much. But with 9/11—and especially with Wolfowitz's and Kagan's articulation of the hardened American position in early 2002—the diverging transatlantic instincts came into increasing conflict. As has been noted often, Europeans grossly underestimated the psychological impact of the 9/11 attacks in triggering that fierce American patriotism that focused America's combined sense of victimhood and unassailable power into a can-do global war on terrorism.

Just as important, however—this the Europeans realized only much later—they initially also misjudged the impact on policy in the new American climate of the passionate, disciplined, and brilliant hawks like Wolfowitz and Kagan who had been toiling for a decade to move American foreign policy precisely in this more Hobbesian, Martian direction.

Here a brief digression is necessary because of the fierce polemics about the neoconservatives that arose later. A clear distinction must be made between those battles of 2003 and the actual policy landscape as the actors perceived it in early 2002. The later spats raged, first, over the arcane issue of whether Leo Strauss was or was not the intellectual father of the neoconservatives, and whether this pre–World War II German émigré and influential professor of philosophy at the University of Chicago was or was not protofascist. The second issue was whether the neoconservatives "hijacked" the Bush administration's foreign policy, or whether they have simply been "demonized" by their adversaries who accuse them of having done so. The first topic was utterly irrelevant to the substance of American foreign policy, the second only marginally relevant. But together they have crowded out substantive debate to a remarkable extent.

Clearly the participants in the first quarrel relished reviving, in a new form, America's old left-right ideological wars and rival conspiracy theories of the 1980s. And a few German and British intellectuals joined in the fun of rehashing all the old arguments about Strauss and the conservative attack on liberalism in Germany in the late 1920s and early 1930s. These exchanges hardly touched on concrete issues of foreign policy in the twenty-first century, though.

The second quarrel was different. If, on the one hand, dissenters from Bush's tough line in foreign policy could establish that the folksy American president had been duped by neoconservatives in his administration (as one version had it), then they could perhaps lure more voters to their point of view without crossing swords with the popular president. On the other hand, if the neoconservatives could cast false accusations as the main issue—and thus turn themselves into victims of slander rather than triumphant victors in the vicious ongoing interagency feuds—they could insist that their position was not a partisan one, but simply the position of all Americans. Any opposition would then be not only anti-neoconservative, but also anti-American. And if Bush hard-liners could imply that their critics blamed the foreign policy direction on "neocons," using the term as a negative code word for Jews, they could brand these critics as both anti-American and anti-Semitic. The spin mattered.[24]

Whatever the spin, it was probably not until late 2002 that European mandarins as a whole sensed the post–9/11 sea change in American policy from status-quo guardianship of stability as practiced during the cold war to revolutionary destabilization of the existing order to create a better world.[25]

The lag in European perceptions of the American shift could be explained in part by the strong inertia of habit. Candidate George W. Bush had, of course, never hinted at any neoconservative radicalism in an electoral campaign in which foreign policy featured seldom and only negatively. Perhaps the best-known preview of a Bush policy was the scorn of future National Security Adviser Condoleezza Rice for nation building in her gibe that the Eighty-Second Airborne doesn't escort children to kindergarten.[26] Europeans had admired the subtlety and delicacy with which President George H. W. Bush had handled German unification and the tectonic changes at the end of the cold war, and they expected the same pragmatism and finesse from his son and his son's advisers, all veterans of the Bush *père* administration. They anticipated that a president with no overseas experience, winner of fewer popular votes than his opponent, and installed in office by a five to four decision of the Supreme Court, would necessarily have to govern in the middle. They had been reassured by Bush's assertion in the campaign, "If we are an arrogant nation, [others will] view us that way, but if we're a humble nation, they'll respect us."[27] The Europeans further counted on a repetition of the familiar pattern, in which a new American president, taking office innocent of foreign policy, in his first year opts for continuity, especially in transatlantic relations. And they knew that Wolfowitz had been rebuked by Bush's chief of staff at the Camp David war council four days after 9/11 for pushing, out of turn, the radical idea of invading Iraq.[28]

European Reactions

The potential split of the two sides of the Atlantic into what would become a titanic clash over the Iraq war was thus initially hidden by the overwhelming western solidarity with the United States in the wake of 9/11. All feared that their own arduously constructed open, trusting societies would now be targeted by that ultimate global nongovernmental organization of suicidal assassins.[29] All pulled together instinctively, not only to declare the 9/11 attack an attack on all NATO members, but also to intensify cooperation among intelligence and police agencies. The British, who had maintained a special Anglo-American intelligence relationship over the years in any case, continued their ties and were especially prized for their analysis. The Germans could fill in some gaps in human intelligence, as distinct from signals intelligence, in Iran and Afghanistan. More immediately, they also gave Washington a clue that led to the arrest of Zacarias

Moussaoui, the alleged twentieth hijacker connected with the 9/11 suicide attacks (even if the Germans suspected that the American agencies already had the same raw intelligence, but were simply too big to have noticed the clue in their overload of data). Even so, the Federal Intelligence Service had to fend off very public American blame for Hamburg's inadvertent hosting of the al Qaeda plotters before the 9/11 strike; its defense consisted primarily of reminding American accusers that it was the United States, not Germany, after all, that let the conspirators receive crucial pilots' training, despite various early warnings.

In further cooperation, the Europeans are allowing American FBI, Coast Guard, or other agents in European ports to inspect containers that are bound for the United States, with no complaints about infringement of sovereignty. Berlin further, eventually, worked out a way around its legal ban on extraditing suspects to any country with a death penalty by getting assurances that any testimony of terrorists so extradited could not be used to secure a death sentence. The fledgling European Central Bank joined with the U.S. Federal Reserve, the Treasury Department, and Wall Street to inject liquidity into markets and contain the financial fallout from the catastrophe. They worked together as well to choke off the worldwide networks of terrorist payments (as Washington dropped its earlier objections to tightening international money-laundering restrictions that it had viewed as setting up unwelcome tax-collection agencies). And to show that other policies would not be held hostage by the fight against terrorism, European governments joined with the United States and other partners to ensure a relaunch of the Doha trade round.

In intra-European reactions, in order to facilitate its own defense in the borderless criminal space terrorists and organized mafias had already created, the European Union adopted an EU-wide arrest warrant. In addition, with reluctance, it dropped its civil-rights compunctions about creating an EU-wide police force and upgraded the old, loose TREVI cooperation of law enforcement agencies into a fledgling Europol.[30]

European coordination in foreign policy was less impressive—and this disarray also served Washington's purposes in giving the United States greater bilateral leverage with each EU member individually. German chancellor Gerhard Schröder's call for a European Union summit right after 9/11 to forge a common approach was rejected by his fellow heads of government. Tony Blair hugged Bush as close as he could in continuing the old Anglo-Saxon special relationship. The Spanish and Italian prime ministers, José María Aznar and Silvio Berlusconi, followed Blair's example as junior partners. President Jacques Chirac chose instead the traditional French approach of being a "foul-weather friend" in demurring from U.S. decisions, while still standing ready to commit troops to American expeditions in the end, perhaps after gaining some modification of the superpower's plans. The European maneuvering sometimes grew farcical, as when Blair planned an intimate strategy dinner with Chirac and Schröder, but the Italian, Spanish, Dutch, and Belgian prime ministers all got wind of it and crashed the party at 10 Downing Street—and the eight remaining wallflowers complained anew that they were being subjected to a directorate of the big players. It was all well and good for pundits to interpret the very different reactions of Blair and Chirac as two different methods aimed at the same goal of restraining the United States from more extreme action—but this was small comfort for those watching the discord among leaders who had repeatedly pledged themselves to a common foreign policy.[31]

Public Opinion

Immediately after the September 11 attacks, sympathy for the Americans doubled Bush's (abysmally low) approval ratings in Europe and overturned the pre-9/11 view of the United States as obstructionist in world treaties. As the American military campaign opened in Afghanistan, 64 percent of French, 61 percent of Germans, 73 percent of Britons, and 83 percent of Americans approved the action.[32] Favorable opinion of Bush's foreign policy shot up in France from 16 percent in August 2001 to 32 percent in April 2002, in Germany from 23 to 35 percent, and in the United Kingdom from 17 to 40 percent (as compared with a rise in American popular approval from 45 to 69 percent). Reflecting the wave of affection for Americans, *Le Monde* famously declared, "Nous sommes tous Américains."[33] Two hundred thousand Berliners gathered spontaneously at the Brandenburg Gate to show their sympathy with America. Chancellor Gerhard Schröder pledged "unlimited solidarity" with the United States and eulogized New York as the whole world's "symbol for millions of emigrants fleeing persecution of life and limb. The symbol of a refuge, the chance to survive and make a new beginning, a promise of hope for the persecuted and the oppressed. The incredible and wonderful world-wide solidarity has a lot to do with this phenomenon."[34] The German embassy in Washington established a charity to aid 9/11 victims and survivors, expecting to attract some tens of thousands of dollars—and was immediately inundated with $42 million in donations. And Tony Blair continued to circumnavigate the globe as an avenging angel, to the ovation of Americans and the embarrassment of Englishmen.

As both opinion surveys and government statements attested, the Europeans were greatly relieved by Bush's initial rejection of what they feared could be a profoundly destabilizing Iraq invasion, especially given the lack of evidence linking secular Baghdad with Islamist al Qaeda terrorists—and by the president's meeting with Islamic leaders in the United States to assure them that Washington did not equate the war on terrorism with a war on Islam and a clash of civilizations. They admired America's spectacular success in forcing on the Pakistani government the hard choice of being either for or against the United States by disavowing the extremist Islamist fanatics on its soil to deprive them of a safe haven. They admired American success at weaning key Pashtun warlords away from supporting Mullah Omar to supporting Mullah Bush, as some of the Afghanis phrased it; in anointing the solid Hamid Karzai as interim Afghan leader; and in deflecting an Indian-Pakistani nuclear clash over Kashmir in the midst of all the other turbulence. They appreciated as well Bush's acceptance of Russian president Vladimir Putin's instant pro-western shift as the American president assembled an international coalition that initially resembled the coalition his father had built for the Gulf War. They approved the softening of the Bush hardliners' presumption that China would be the inevitable adversary; and they certainly applauded Bush's increase in previously neglected development aid in the $5 billion Millennium Challenge Account. Both sides of the Atlantic, it seemed, were agreed that the most important task was to drain the swamps that bred terrorists.

They were clearly disappointed when Washington spurned NATO's offer of help beyond commissioning a European task force to monitor the waters off the Horn of Africa, letting a few alliance AWACS surveillance planes patrol North America to free U.S. counterparts for missions in

Southeast Asia, and accepting some European special forces and marines for Operation Enduring Freedom in Afghanistan. But in the first few months after 9/11, misgivings were secondary. The general European assessment was that Bush's response was measured—and that the administration now felt a need for partners and was returning from the flamboyant unilateralism of its first eight months to a more traditional post–World War II multilateralism.

Most striking in this transatlantic solidarity, perhaps, was the role that Chancellor Schröder, a child of the "1968" anti–Vietnam War left, played in sending German special forces to fight alongside American troops in Afghanistan. Defying all the semipacifist traditions of his party and his Green Party coalition partners, he staked his chancellery post on a vote of nonconfidence on the issue, and he won. For the first time since 1945, German troops were sent into combat outside Europe.

The American Narrative

In retrospect, however, the Europeans should probably not have been as surprised as they were by the direction the Bush administration ultimately took. Not only had the American and European self-images been diverging for some time and, after 9/11, offering authentic superpatriotic veins on the western side of the Atlantic for the neoconservatives to tap. Even more conspicuously, the neoconservatives had never hidden the radical agenda they began pressing in earnest after 9/11. The dispute still rages, of course, over just how much of U.S.-European tension should be attributed to unconsonant long-term trends on the two sides of the ocean (and by extrapolation to preexistent "anti-Americanism") and how much derives from Bush policies alone (and therefore represents, from the U.S. point of view, an "anti-Bushism" that is less structural and less dangerous).

Certainly in the perceived American narrative—and never more so than after 9/11—the identity of the United States is that of the city set on a hill. America is uniquely righteous, and uniquely justified in its policies, because it has the best democracy in the world, and, along with it, the best absorption of foreign immigrants. Europeans, by contrast, are widely dismissed by American elites (if less so by the man on the street, the workhorse Chicago Council on Foreign Relations surveys suggest)[35] as rigid, weak, spoiled, pusillanimous, and free riders on America's provision of the public good of global security. And especially with the fusion of the American religious right and Jewish neoconservatives in backing Israel's hard-line suppression of the second *intifada* and of Palestinians who might be harboring terrorists, American commentators have regularly accused the Europeans of veiled or not-so-veiled anti-Semitism in their criticism of the Israeli approach.

Since the U.S. system is the world's best, if the American government selected by that system decides on certain policies, then these must logically also be the best policies for the world, whether they involve the taken-for-granted extraterritoriality of the Sarbanes-Oxley bill on mandatory accounting practices in business, the effort to go beyond mere U.S. abstention from the International Criminal Court to pressure other countries to reject it, or the refusal to pay U.S. dues to UN programs in which any information is disseminated about abortion.[36]

Moreover, the United States has recently been uniquely successful economically. Its productivity increase soars above Europe's.[37] The United States was the motor for the extraordinary boom of the 1990s, and even after the bubble burst, the United States continued to lead the world as the consumer of last resort. When U.S. stock exchanges plunge, European bourses plunge as well; when Wall Street rallies, so do Frankfurt, London, and Amsterdam. Today no one would dream of repeating President Jimmy Carter's plea of the 1970s by demanding that deflationary Japan or anemic Europe become the new locomotive of the world economy.

Finally, Americans know that they are uniquely powerful. Their smart munitions and real-time battlefield intelligence and management have raced so far ahead in the revolution in military affairs that few allies are well enough equipped technologically to fight alongside them. Their annual dollar outlay for defense is double that of all European Union members taken together. Yet the September 11, 2001, felling of the World Trade Towers, followed by the still-unsolved anthrax attacks, shattered Americans' illusion of invulnerability and left the superpower with the volatile mixed feelings of omnipotence and vulnerability that Pierre Hassner has dissected[38]—and with the perception of more threats from international terrorism and potential Iraqi development of nuclear weapons than the Europeans saw.[39] Europeans, having contained their own cults of domestic terrorism in the 1970s and 1980s, might think that

U.S. alarm is exaggerated, but Americans, targeted by global terrorists and swept up in their righteous war on evil and their swift victory in Iraq, feel that Europeans still hide behind the United States and willfully underestimate the dangers of fanatics' acquisition of weapons of mass destruction (WMD).

One more element in America's sense of power derives from Washington's military and economic clout but goes well beyond it. That is the U.S. capacity to set the global agenda. If the Bush administration decides it will deploy a missile-defense system, then after a few months, opposition to this program evaporates around the world. If the United States decides to torpedo the International Criminal Court, the Europeans eventually stop wasting their political capital on opposing exemptions for U.S. personnel. If the United States, for whatever reason, takes its case for invading Iraq to the United Nations, the whole burden of proof rests not on establishing compelling arguments in favor of an extraordinary resort to war, but rather on the need for allies to demonstrate their loyalty to the United States and to its chosen course.

The European Narrative

The European self-image is strikingly different from the American one, as Kagan, Cooper, and Weiler all stress. After centuries of armed conflict, the Europeans see themselves as having finally attained the miracle of peace in their once war-prone heartland—not least through the benign intervention of the United States in World Wars I and II and the Marshall Plan, of course.[40] They were shocked and chastened by the forty-five million dead in World War II, most of them in Europe. And between 1945 and the mid-1990s they responded with a chain reaction of reconciliations so fundamental that today younger Germans and French simply cannot comprehend how their grandparents ever considered each other arch-enemies; Dutch who originally protested Princess Beatrix's marriage to a German mourned the death of their beloved Prince Claus in 2002; Poles flock to seek jobs and education in the Berlin most of their parents despised and feared; and younger Ukrainians, despite Polish-Ukrainian butchery that continued even after World War II, see rapidly modernizing Poland as an attractive model and their lifeline to the West.

Even the "German question" that had dogged Europe for the century and a half before 1945—the conundrum of how to integrate the populous, energetic Germans in peace with their neighbors—turned out to have been solved quietly in the second half of the twentieth century. By the end of the cold war no country was more keen than Germany on reconciliation and the progressive subordination of national to European identity. Yet long after unified Germany's main problem became weakness rather than strength in the late 1990s, the reflex of many British and American commentators to events in Berlin would still be to ask if Germany was once more becoming too "assertive."[41] For insight into the shift in German mentality, credit must go to Swiss journalist Fritz René Allemann for being the first to trust the historical change and to write boldly *Bonn Ist Nicht Weimar* (Bonn Is Not Weimar) as early as 1956.[42] No prominent German historian believed the evidence of transformation sufficiently to attempt a comprehensive reinterpretation of pre-Hitler history as laying the groundwork for eventual rejection by Germany of its prolonged antiwestern *sonderweg* [exceptionalism] and metamorphosis into a "normal" country until Heinrich August Winkler published *Der lange Weg nach Westen* (The Long Road to the West) in 2000.[43] Even then numerous German critics faulted their compatriot for his rush to positive judgment. The magisterial five-volume history of the Federal Republic of (West) Germany that was published shortly before German unification still would not venture such a benign evaluation.[44] It ended instead with the essay "Die deutsche Frage: Das offene Dilemma" ("The German Question: The Open Dilemma"). Timothy Garton Ash's thoughtful *In Europe's Name*, published in 1993, hedged its bets somewhat in making the case that the Federal Republic consistently pursued its own interests, all the while invoking "Europe's name."[45] Yet the obverse of this had to be that all along Bonn's self-definition of enlightened German interests was remarkably pro-European.[46]

The first real test of European Community robustness came with the end of the cold war. Until then its institutions, however odd, had worked well enough. A consensus system in an entity that was far more than a confederation but far less than a federation should have been a recipe for scapegoating, torpor, lowest-common-denominator gridlock, and blackmail by the most ornery members of the club, à la Malta in the 1970s negotiations at the Conference on Security and Cooperation in Europe. In that forum Valletta repeatedly waited until all three dozen other participants had laboriously worked out a general compromise, then refused to sign off on the agreement until it won some unrelated parochial concession. In the EC/EU, to be sure, almost every member government succumbed on occasion (usually during elections) to blaming "Brussels" for domestic troubles. And every member government constantly chafes under the policy straitjacket it is forced into by having well over half its domestic legislation prescribed by the EU.

Nonetheless, the system of shaming recalcitrants into consensus, if necessary, has functioned passably well. The EC/EU has always muddled through. The European Commission acts authoritatively in negotiating on behalf of all EU members on trade issues and enforcing antitrust regulations. Cooperation turns out not to have been just an emergency reaction to the Soviet threat, nor even a construct that still depends on the offshore balancing of the Germans by the United States. After the cold-war threat vanished, a quickened European Community still took major steps toward fulfilling its original goal of a real single market, by 1992. The following year it renamed itself the European Union (in an appellation that reflected noble intent rather more than reality). Thereafter, in a historically unprecedented move, twelve EU members even ceded one of the most precious attributes of sovereignty in abandoning their national currencies to a common euro—and in the process invented best-practice benchmarking as the way to escape the lowest common denominator. Most impressive of all in this exercise, perhaps, was the real economic convergence that occurred among major national economies, especially in low inflation.

No less astounding has been the success of the EC/EU in the help it rendered the new democracies, market economies, and civil societies to the east in their impossibly accelerated decade-long race through the political, economic, and social revolutions the west Europeans took more than a century to master. Unlike the agonizing death of the Ottoman Empire a century earlier—a bloody precedent that fueled fears about what the end of Russian empire might bring—the Soviet implosion was remarkably peaceful. Only in Romania in the external empire was there a spasm of violence. Only in Chechnya in the internal empire was there sustained violence. In Europe proper the atrocities in former Yugoslavia in the early 1990s were eventually halted (with the reluctant aid of the United States, of course, and after five years of paralysis by both Europe and the United States), and for the first time in their history the Balkans too came to be included in the penumbra of western Europe's haven of peace and prosperity. The entry into the EU club of ten new central European countries in an arc from Poland to Slovenia in 2004 will mark these lands' "return" (occasionally real, more often concocted, in a normative rewriting of history) to the West.

All told, the EU role in the transition has been a significant exercise in crisis management and even—as Germans like to point out to American critics—of regime change on a huge scale, executed peacefully. Ironically, precisely because it has been so successful, it has drawn little attention. It radiates no aura to help shield the European experiment in new forms of governance from two existential challenges that now confront it simultaneously. The first is the adjustment of EU institutions and procedures as the club welcomes central Europeans who have barely been socialized into pluralist and democratic give-and-take, let alone into the delicate EU consensus system. The second is potential hostility to the European project from the very U.S. patron that originally forced the resistant Europeans to cooperate as a prerequisite for receiving Marshall Plan aid.

The Neoconservative Narrative

In early 2003 the final position of American neoconservatives on Europe was not completely clear. But there were warning signals.

Neoconservatives, as Americans know and Europeans have been learning, are policy activists who typically started as Democrats but turned into Republicans in the 1970s or, specifically, into Reagan Republicans in the 1980s, because they advocated a harder line on the Soviet Union and arms control than the Democrats did. Many were equally hard-line on Israeli-Palestinian issues. Many would move into key policymaking positions in the administration of George W. Bush. Richard Perle, who as an aide to Democratic senator Henry Jackson had masterminded passage of the Jackson-Vanik amendment limiting American cooperation with the Soviet Union as long as Soviet Jews were not allowed free emigration, became chairman (later, ordinary member) of the influential Defense Policy Board. Lewis Libby became chief of staff to Vice President Dick Cheney. Douglas Feith became under secretary of defense for policy, John Bolton under secretary of state for arms control and international security.

The neoconservatives in the new Bush administration, who were primarily interested in foreign policy, formed a highly compatible marriage with the domestic Republican right to build an intellectual worldview that was far more coherent than in most U.S. administrations. The party right saw in the Republican capture of both the White House and Congress the chance of a century, an opportunity to roll back the whole governmental and political legacy of Franklin Delano Roosevelt's New Deal and Lyndon B. Johnson's Great Society. Some components of the desired reversal, such as tax cuts for the rich to promote investment and deregulation, reflected long-time Republican orthodoxy. Others, such as abandonment of the balanced budget that Republicans had long championed and Democratic president Clinton had finally achieved—and a return plunge into large deficits to finance the huge new appropriations for the military and home defense—were highly unorthodox. To critics and fans alike they seemed to be designed to create a future financial crisis that could be solved only by cutting social entitlements.[47] Not quite as unorthodox, for a party whose bête noir had long been big government but whose pet domestic issue was strict law and order, was the expansion of intrusive government powers of investigation and police control in the war on terrorism.

Such domestic issues held no intrinsic interest for Europeans, but they were important insofar as they bolstered the neoconservative foreign policy.

By all accounts, the opening salvos of the American neoconservatives' campaign to revise America's foreign policy began with Charles Krauthammer's article "The Unipolar Moment" in *Foreign Affairs* in 1990 and Wolfowitz's draft Defense Policy Guidance in 1992.[48] Krauthammer christened the postwar era "unipolar," in a phrase that stuck. Wolfowitz, then under secretary of defense for planning, planted the seeds of preemption that would eventually blossom into the National Security Strategy of September 2002 and the Iraq war of 2003. Wolfowitz had in any case opposed the decision of President George H. W. Bush to end the Gulf War in 1991 after ousting the Iraqi army from Kuwait without marching on to Baghdad to depose Saddam Hussein. The policy guidance draft that he supervised (and that was written by a team that included

Lewis Libby) revisited this issue in envisaging U.S. military intervention in general "as a constant fixture" and in Iraq in particular whenever it might be needed to ensure "access to vital raw material, primarily Persian Gulf oil." The underlying global philosophy was that the United States must ensure its own military dominance in the world by "deterring potential competitors from even aspiring to a larger regional or global role." China seemed to be the main suspect, but a few European readers of the draft could not help but wonder if they appeared somewhere on the list too. Preemptive attacks and ad hoc coalitions were among the favored means to preserve American supremacy.[49]

When the contents of the Wolfowitz memorandum were leaked to the *New York Times*, there was an outcry among more conventional Washington political actors that led to its rejection and adoption of a much more cautious final Pentagon document.

The next neoconservative foreign-policy declarations of note came in 1996, in the United States and also in Israel. Kagan and *Weekly Standard* editor William Kristol called in *Foreign Affairs* for a "neo-Reaganite foreign policy" that would apply America's military might "unabashedly" to advance political liberalization in a "benevolent hegemony."[50] Perle, Feith, and David Wurmser (who would become a senior adviser to John Bolton at the State Department) wrote a report to the newly elected Likud government urging it to make "a clean break" with peace negotiations with the Palestinians and with the whole notion of exchanging land for peace. They advocated instead "reestablishing the principle of preemption"— and hoped that Israel might even "roll back" Syria, promote the ouster of Iraqi leader Saddam Hussein, and thus "affect the strategic balance in the Middle East profoundly."[51]

A year later the neoconservatives founded the Project for the New American Century under the chairmanship of Kristol; cofounder Kagan was on the board. In January 1998, Wolfowitz, Perle, Bolton, and Rumsfeld joined twelve other prominent conservatives who would staff the top ranks of the future Bush administration in signing an open letter condemning the containment of Iraq as a failure and urging President Clinton to "aim at the removal of Saddam Hussein's regime from power."

Two years thereafter, the project's "Rebuilding America's Defenses" noted the problems raised by stationing of American soldiers in Saudi

Arabia and hinted at Iraq as a better venue in recommending a permanent U.S. military presence in the Gulf even "should Saddam pass from the scene."[52]

Europe figured very little in the various statements. NATO was mentioned in a cursory, but not unfriendly fashion. The ad hoc coalitions that were to aid the United States in the Middle East could well have been understood in the contemporary context as appropriate for that region without carrying any implications for the permanent European alliance.

Immediately after the 9/11 attacks—within days of Wolfowitz's rebuff at Camp David—thirty-seven leading associates of the Project for the New American Century wrote an open letter again advocating military intervention in Iraq, observing, "Even if evidence does not link Iraq directly to the attack, any strategy aiming at the eradication of terrorism and its sponsors must include a determined effort to remove Saddam Hussein from power."[53]

A clash between neoconservatives and Europeans was by no means predestined. But it was an incident that was waiting to happen.

CHAPTER TWO

POX AMERICANA?

2002 Polemics

As EUROPEANS ABSORBED the double blow of Bush's "axis of evil" shot and
Wolfowitz's scorn for permanent coalitions in early 2002, the transatlantic
polemics broke out, over both policy substance and what the Europeans
had come to regard in previous decades as their right to a voice in Washington's decisionmaking.

The immediate trigger was the resurgence of American talk, in the
glow of the quick military triumph in Afghanistan, about finishing at long
last the job begun by Bush senior and overthrowing Iraqi strongman Saddam Hussein. Now it seemed that earlier European relief over Bush's
rejection of war on an Iraq not known to have either links to al Qaeda or
usable nuclear weapons might have been a gross misreading of Washington. There was as yet no specific plan or timetable for taking out the Iraqi
leader, but all the decade-old neoconservative summonses to war on Iraq
were again being rehearsed in the American media. And this drive in turn
raised questions about what voice the Europeans might have in any risky
expedition in a Mesopotamian environment that was likely to be far more
hostile than Afghanistan had been.

Collegial Hegemony?

Issues of substance and procedure were thus intertwined from the start.
The Europeans, including the British at this stage, clearly wanted a say in
America's war councils in order to discourage the war, given the lack of
any compelling reason for it. The Bush administration, just as clearly, had
no intention of giving any Europeans a voice that might foreclose the

option of war. In any case, the continental Europeans were thought to have no right to give advice, since they had so little to offer militarily.

The most succinct description of the struggle that was now shaping up in the western alliance might be that Europeans fully accepted American hegemony, as they had for the past half century—but that they wanted that hegemony to be conducted in the collegial way they had gotten used to during the cold war. It took an Englishman, Chris Patten, speaking in Europe's name as the European commissioner for external relations but invoking in his own person the Anglo-Saxon special relationship, to dare to speak out first.

In a pained essay on the opinion page of the *Financial Times* a fortnight after the Munich Security Conference in February 2002, Patten prefaced his plea by saying that he had not "one drop of anti-Americanism flowing through [his] veins." But, added the one-time Tory chairman and last British governor of Hong Kong, "True friends are not sycophants. Those of us who are concerned at certain trends in US policymaking have a duty to speak up. The unilateralist urge is not new. Nor is it ignoble," he granted. Yet

> it is ultimately ineffective and self-defeating. . . . The stunning and unexpectedly rapid success of the military campaign in Afghanistan was a tribute to American capacity. But it has perhaps reinforced some dangerous instincts: that the projection of military power is the only basis of true security; that the US can rely only on itself; and that allies may be useful as an optional extra but that the US is big and strong enough to manage without them if it must. As the world's only superpower, the US carries a particular responsibility to maintain moral authority for her leadership. "America's challenge is to transfer its power into moral consensus, promoting its values not by imposition but by their willing acceptance in a world that, for all its seeming resistance, desperately needs enlightening leadership." That sentence is not mine but the final paragraph of a recent book by Henry Kissinger.[1]

In case anyone missed the point, one-time New Labour theorist Will Hutton brought a more acerbic pen to the same themes. "The most important political story of our time is the rise of the American Right and the near collapse of American liberalism. This has transformed the political and cultural geography of the United States," Hutton began.

It takes extraordinary circumstances to produce the kind of warnings voiced over the last week by Chris Patten, . . . but these circumstances are extraordinary. Patten has damned the emerging US reliance on its fantastic military superiority over all other nations to pursue what it wants as it wants as an "absolutist and simplistic" approach to the rest of the world that is ultimately self-defeating. It is also intellectually and morally wrong. He is the first ranking British politician to state so boldly what has been a commonplace in France and Germany for weeks. The most obvious flashpoint is the weight of evidence that after Afghanistan George Bush intends a massive military intervention to topple Iraq's Saddam Hussein. Dangerous dictator he may be, but the unilateral decision to declare war upon another state without a casus belli other than suspicion will upset the fabric of law on which international relations rests, as well as destabilising the Middle East. . . . US unilateralism is uncompromisingly absolutist because it is ideological, which is what makes it so dangerous. American conservatism . . . unites patriotism, unilateralism, the celebration of inequality and the right of a moral élite to rule into a single unifying ideology.[2]

Yet another Englishman, Charles Grant, founder and president of the Centre for European Reform, wrote, "Since victory in Afghanistan, the Bush administration seems to have reverted to unbridled, right-wing unilateralism. It has scrapped the ABM treaty, supported Ariel Sharon's attacks on the Palestinian Authority and, in the treatment of prisoners held in Cuba, has been cavalier in its observance of the Geneva Conventions." He quoted a "senior figure in the British ministry of defence, a deeply pro-American institution," as saying in January 2002: "'In order to help the US war effort, we are spending large amounts of money . . . and we are putting the lives of our special forces at risk. And yet, in return, the Americans do not listen to a word we say and frequently create difficulties, whether on the organisation of the peacekeeping force in Kabul or any other military matter. I have to ask whether it is in the national interest that we should go on offering such unstinting support."[3]

In their quick sketches, Patten, Hutton, and Grant pointed to some of the substantive policies of the hegemon that troubled Britons and continentals alike: the "dangerous instinct" that "military power is the only basis of true security," disdain for international law, American "absolutism," "unbridled, right-wing unilateralism," and loss of "moral authority." But what they most wanted to address was the immediate procedural issue of the structure and nature of future relations between the United States and its democratic allies. This question was "procedural," of course, only in the sense that rule of law is procedural—but at the same time is the foundation without which rights and democracy cannot exist.

If the American hegemon intended to rule by bullying the rest of the world, including its European allies, Patten was suggesting, this would seriously erode trust in the United States by its friends and, by implication, their willingness to follow American leadership. If, however, Washington would exercise its leadership in the world as a lawmaker and constructer of cooperative institutions, America could retain its precious store of existing trust and the readiness of its allies to follow the path blazed by the United States. And success in the quest that was the absolute U.S. priority, defeat of terrorists and rogue states that might acquire weapons of mass destruction, would depend above all on nurturing that confidence in America that would persuade others to help in the hunt because they themselves want the security that America wants.

For Europeans the litmus test of U.S. conduct in this area would be the use or abuse of transatlantic allies, especially in such issues as unilateralism, international law, respect for strong inherited inhibitions on resort to war, and care of institutions that discipline and outlive personal and even power relationships.

Post–World War II Leadership

In this context what Patten meant by counseling America to "maintain moral authority for her leadership" was to seek the same sort of widespread approval of U.S. aims by others that Washington had enjoyed during the cold-war years. In that period, even at the height of anti–Vietnam War sentiment, no allied (non-French) European government had ever fundamentally contested U.S. primacy—and the Soviet threat was only part of the reason for this internalized constraint. Even in the midst of the periodic rows about burden sharing, or forward defense, or deployments, all the European allies were reassured rather than frightened by knowing that at the end of the day the United States, as formal primus inter pares in NATO, could force decisions on the alliance. This made for one of the striking differences between NATO and the European Community, in which historical suspicions and the approximately equal weight of the four biggest members meant no one could ever compel closure, and issues could drag on for years without resolution. The sense of the cold-war relationship was summed up in the bon mot that the Europeans loved to be led by the Americans—as long as it was in the direction the Europeans wanted to go.

In theory, important decisions by NATO had to be unanimous. In practice, of course, the United States could secure almost any course of alliance action it really desired. Yet the presumption of prior discussion and consultation was no façade. Policies were wrestled out, and modified, to meet major concerns of members. NATO's Military Committee worked with input from all contributing nations to translate political directives into sensible force planning and to generate scenarios. Within the integrated military command, top slots were distributed in what was broadly viewed as an equitable fashion. And over the years, the joint exercises and unprecedented circulation within the club of each country's medium-term procurement programs produced such transparency, it was said, that never again would a member be able to surprise its allies with the kind of lightning raid the British and French conducted when they temporarily seized the Suez Canal back from Egypt in 1956.

Even in that most sensitive of all issues, contingency planning for nuclear use, nonnuclear NATO members got to share in the existential agonizing of the alliance's Nuclear Planning Group. One of the reasons the realist school of political science would be proved so wrong in anticipating that unified Germany would naturally go nuclear once the country regained full sovereignty in 1990 was precisely that for decades the Federal Republic had had a reasonable say in the grisly potential employment of the American nuclear weapons that guaranteed Europe's longest peace in history.[4] "Forward defense," stationing of battlefield and medium-range nuclear weapons, and the war gaming of nuclear use all occasioned fierce German-American fights—but no one questioned the right of the front-line Germans to argue their preferences forcefully and to have them taken into account. However great the asymmetries between the U.S. super-power and the German political dwarf, the Americans still encouraged their German protégés to speak their minds in alliance circles.

To be sure, during the cold war there were frequent European com-plaints about too little consultation or the poor quality of dialogue with Washington. But so ingrained was the expectation of joint working of problems that the principle of consultation itself was a given and was assumed to benefit all participants, including the hegemon.

Indeed, the whole consultative network of entangling institutions that sprang up in the wake of World War II was invented not by a devastated Europe that sought to constrain the U.S. colossus, but by the U.S. colos-sus itself. Then as now, America was the world's sole superpower. It disposed of the world's only atom bombs and produced between a third and a half of the world economy, as compared with some 27 percent today.[5] Reluctantly, the United States inherited the Pax Britannica and took over responsibility for maintaining the public good of freedom of the high seas, from piracy and for trade. In the hair-trigger nuclear age, the new Pax Americana did not perpetuate London's balancing of shifting European powers, but—once Moscow too acquired the bomb—consisted of keeping a stable bipolar balance of terror, while defending Western Europe against Soviet pressure through the NATO military shield, nation (re)building, and economic quickening.

Since American citizens had little stomach for the burdens of extended imperial rule on the old British pattern, Washington's choice of a partic-ipatory hegemony made sense. In retrospect, the arrangements turned out to have been much more efficient than any starkly hierarchical world order would have been. The dense cooperative network of NATO, the nascent European Community, the World Bank, the International Mon-etary Fund, and even the United Nations required only minimal U.S. maintenance. Far from being weakened by voluntarily sharing its power and influence with its client states, the American hegemon gained vastly more from energizing its partners' imagination and initiatives to promote the common good than it would have won by extracting sullen obedience.

The United Nations may have disappointed Washington's grander political hopes for this body—in part from cold-war stalemate, in part from a rigid concept of sovereignty as the world splintered into ever more ministates of varying democratic or authoritarian provenance—and settled down to become a channel for humanitarian assistance and a forum for world opinion. But the interlocking western institutions flourished, took on a life of their own, and matured into a supranational system of what political scientists would later call governance. Within this voluntary system, the United States rarely had to resort to raw coercion and, to the constant perplexity of realists, never provoked the kind of "balancing" of Lilliputians against the regnant Gulliver that hegemons in the past had always encountered.[6]

In the early post–World War II years the relief of the smaller countries liberated from the Nazi yoke at America's continued off-shore balancing of the Germans (and the Russians, of course) could be taken as a given. A more open question was the eventual attitude of the "great powers" of Britain and France, since the obverse of American dominance was their own decline. That issue was settled in 1956, when the United States compelled British and French forces to hand the Suez Canal back to Egypt. With this confrontation, nostalgia for former greatness yielded to realism in London, if not in Paris. A decade later President Charles de Gaulle pulled out of NATO's American-led integrated military command (to the subsequent regret of French military officers, who felt deprived of command slots and access to the NATO standard of equipment, training, and tactics). Thereafter the French sustained their pride with Paris's inflated role (given the French wartime collaboration with the Nazis) in wielding a UN Security Council veto, having an occupation zone in West Berlin and West Germany, and acquiring nuclear weapons, with the ultrasecret help of the Americans.

As for Germany, one of the most striking aspects of America's postwar innovations was Washington's rejection of traditional victor's justice of the kind that had led to the punitive Versailles Treaty after World War I—and to its sequel war within a generation. The United States discarded the Morgenthau Plan, which would have razed the industry of the defeated German enemy and left it only pastures and cropland. It quickly rehabilitated the West German successor state, in part to form a bulwark against Soviet pressures, and at the cost of a premature end to denazification. One of its unanticipated rewards was the popular affection for the American occupiers, especially after the 1948–49 airlift supplied the besieged West Berliners with eight thousand tons a day of potatoes and meat and coal, and even, once, a live camel. Still today Christian Democratic deputy parliamentary leader Wolfgang Schäuble speaks for his countrymen in exclaiming, "Thank God!" that America has been the hegemon all these years.[7]

German gratitude increased too as the Federal Republic was included as a full beneficiary of Marshall Plan aid. U.S. magnanimity and enlightened self-interest in donating $12 billion to spur European recovery—and hasten the time when the old continent would again become America's commercial competitor—marked another historical innovation. And so did the preconditions that required the squabbling European nations to agree on a joint plan for distribution of the largesse before any one of them could receive a penny. This compulsory cooperation laid the foundation for the first transnational European Coal and Steel Community to prevent Germany from unilateral exploitation of what were still the prime raw materials of war—and for the maturing of the ECSC into the European Community and eventually the European Union, as the largest multination zone of peace and prosperity in the world.

All in all, the creative American approach was a breathtaking departure from what would soon be labeled, as the nuclear age adopted the new paradigm of game theory, zero-sum thinking. It was a storybook illustration of Nye's sense of using soft power to persuade others to want what you want.

The whole structure was an imaginative response to the puzzle that confronts all victors after major wars, contends Georgetown's G. John Ikenberry—the conundrum of how to organize optimally the uneven power of nations that emerge from catastrophic breakdowns of previous world orders.

The leading state—driven by a basic incentive to conserve its power—wants a legitimate order that will reduce its requirements to coerce. The greater the asymmetries of power after the war, the more this circumstance should be at the front of the leading state's postwar thinking. Likewise, the sharper the power asymmetries, the more weaker and secondary states will be worried about domination and [its obverse of] abandonment. This is where the possibility for an institutional bargain enters, particularly if other circumstances exist that allow states to be confident that institutions will in fact restrain power and lock in policy commitments.... [T]he leading state agrees to restrain its own potential for domination and abandonment in exchange for greater compliance by subordinate states. Both sides are better off with a constitutional order than in an order based on the constant threat of the indiscriminate and arbitrary exercise of power.[8]

In other words, legitimacy that is accepted by others is the cheapest and most effective way for a hegemon to rule.

Such abstract conjecture would have been alien to Secretary of State Dean Acheson, of course. He was a craftsman, not an articulator of visions. His memoirs of his cohort's experiments as World War II segued into the cold war sound like nothing so much as a fireman's methodical listing of the alarms on his watch and the means by which each conflagration was mastered, whether by water jet or chemical suppressant or counterfire. Decisions were repeatedly made, as Acheson ruefully phrased it, out of "ignorance of the true situation, daring, and buoyant determination." The most he allowed himself was the conclusion that "Our efforts for the most part left conditions better than we found them"—and that his colleagues might well "feel in their hearts that it was nobly done."[9]

Indeed, the structures Acheson and his cohort bequeathed their successors, defying all expectations, would endure for half a century. As the cold war collapsed in 1990, these structures still set the pattern for what many central Europeans regarded as the miracle of the virtually bloodless end of the Russian empire. Bush 41,[10] trusting today's Germans in these institutions in a way the British and French did not, forced the latter to acquiesce in the reunification of West and East Germany. Soviet president Mikhail Gorbachev approved—preferring to lock united Germany into a NATO dominated by the United States rather than take the risk that an unattached Germany might become a loose cannon. Only in Romania and in the European periphery of the former Yugoslavia was there a paroxysm of killing.[11]

However improvised, this whole process of creating the transatlantic community in the first dozen years after World War II was reminiscent of the historical emergence of rule of law as an organizing principle in protodemocratic and then democratic domestic societies.[12] At least this was the continuity the Europeans sensed in their whole escape from Hitler's nightmare.

The Arguments

Watching their mentors in democracy scupper the very paradigm of international law in favor of raw power in the twenty-first century, as it seemed to many, was traumatic, especially for the Germans. "Everything I believe in regarding peace, freedom, and respect for law, I have learned from the Americans—and so have all my German colleagues," commented Humboldt University law professor Ingolf Pernice sadly as the Iraq war that he opposed broke out.[13] The more pragmatic British might dismiss such theorizing as unnecessary baggage; the more ideational Germans could not, especially since precepts of democracy and law were a core part of the new identity they embraced as they transmuted the old national will not to know about Nazi atrocities into a compulsion for individual vigilance.

In retrospective soft focus, the half century of the cold war looked like a lost golden age in the transatlantic marriage, despite all the old quarrels. By 2002 the Europeans were coming to realize that even the successful completion of the Afghan campaign would not, after all, bring a return to participatory hegemony. The style of Wolfowitz and Rumsfeld—and it was indeed the Defense Department, not the State Department, that was running Bush's foreign policy—was instead hierarchical. Washington would make unilateral decisions; it would be up to the Europeans to follow if they wished—or become irrelevant if they did not. This subordination rankled.

At the same time, Europe's insubordination as expressed by Patten in February 2002 rankled the American neoconservatives. If Patten's manner suggested a reproachful elder brother, Richard Perle's manner in rebutting him suggested a crusading prosecutor. Perle, who has reveled in baiting British "wets"[14] ever since he took on a hostile audience at the London School of Economics in the midst of the Cuban missile crisis at the ten-der age of nineteen, challenged the European commissioner's authority and mocked Patten's profession of affection for America.

"Mr Patten has not been elected to public office since 1987 and is responsible to no one," the nonelected Perle observed, coolly dismissing the right of the European commissioner to speak for Europeans, since he had been only appointed, and not elected, to his post. "What Mr Patten fails to appreciate is that the President is speaking overwhelmingly for the American people" in "describing some of the nastiest regimes of the 20th and 21st centuries" as the "axis of evil."

Besides, stated Perle, "It is patronising of Mr Chris Patten to emphasise how much he loves and admires America and then to embark on a foreign policy prescription that would leave us vulnerable to terrorism. . . . [E]very time Europe gets into trouble, it phones the United States for help. Europe is so weak and in disarray on so many security issues, it cannot do anything without American assistance."

Furthermore, when British foreign secretary Jack Straw goes to Tehran, he does so "to kiss the behinds of the mullahs," as "Mr Patten [too] would like to do."[15]

When the two protagonists met face to face some months later on the podium of the American Enterprise Institute, where Perle is a resident fellow, Perle was more civil in demeanor, if just as resolute in substance. Their debate is worth quoting at some length, since it encapsulates all the issues deriving from the basic feuds over unilateralism, militarization of foreign policy, and the dearth of allied consultations that were now roiling the transatlantic relationship.

Patten opened the debate by proposing that three major questions were coming together simultaneously: first, "how the rest of us deal with the United States, and how the United States deals with the rest of us"; second, the danger that Samuel Huntington's thesis of a clash of civilizations might now become self-fulfilling; and third, "how we can deal with the new challenges to international governance and the rule of law."

Patten elaborated on the second issue by commenting, "I think the degree of antipathy in the Islamic world to the West is very worrying. Of course hatred of America is wholly, wholly unjustified, but if I was an American I'm not sure that I would necessarily feel that it could be best dealt with by bombing the haters. And I have to say in passing that I've always been rather sceptical about the proposition that military action in the Gulf is the best way of making the whole region more moderate and the best way of making the whole region believe rather more passionately in Jeffersonian democracy."

In addressing U.S. views on these issues, Patten noted,

For some years now in the United States there has been a new school of thought, I think increasingly influential, of which Richard has been a pellucid luminary. And it is a school of thought which has challenged the liberal internationalism and indeed the Realpolitik internationalism (think of the first President Bush of the post–cold war years). . . . It's a school of thought which strongly opposed the Madrid and the Oslo peace processes in the Middle East, a school of thought which believed that [former Israeli prime minister] Benjamin Netanyahu was a wimp because he went along with some of those peace processes. A school of thought which argued in one or two cases that the Palestinians should be driven out of the West Bank—to borrow a phrase from a member of the present Administration, that the West Bank should be 'detoxified.' Above all it is a school of thought which believed that any multilateralism undermines America's sovereignty and America's ability to stand up for its own interests. . . .

The atrocities of September 11th seem to have convinced these distinguished unilateralists that they've been right all along. . . . But are we [Europeans] wholly wrong to think that the 11th September made international co-operation more important, not less? That the 11th September should have made us realise that technological and military force don't and won't ever provide the whole answer if we want to live in a safer world. It's interesting . . . that that remains the view of the great majority of the American public. . . .[O]utside the beltway, in the rest of America, in the mainstreets, Americans are just as multilateralist, just as supportive of the UN, just as supportive of working with the international community as they've ever been.

In reply, Perle again took Europe to task for its military weakness and for its constantly repeated "cliché" that the use of force "must always be the last resort" and the concomitant "foolish, dangerous and costly [indulgence] in a prolonged period of ineffective political and economic measures."

Perle also rejected Patten's "stereotype" in referring to "a new neo-conservative 'school' that is challenging some established notions about foreign and defense policy. . . . The idea that there is a school, a group of people, who believe that any multilateralism is hostile to American interests is simply wrong. We hear it all the time and the repetition of it only confuses matters."[16] He also objected to Patten's "suggestion that the 'laws must apply to everyone' as though the United States were lawless and we did not agree that laws should apply to us." It would be difficult "to cite an example in which the United States has acted outside the law. Even the contemplated military action in Iraq, were it to take place, would take place entirely within the structure of International Law, Article 51 of the United Nations' Charter, for example which acknowledges—does not confer but acknowledges—the right of self defence."

Perle closed with:

> A word or two about unilateralism and self defence. Clearly the most difficult issue straining the relationship between the United States and much of the world, has to do with the American attitude towards Iraq. And the charge is that if we were to act militarily, we would be acting in a unilateral manner. But everyone recognises the right of self defence. The question then is: is the danger from Saddam Hussein to the United States of such imminence that we are justified in invoking the concept of self defence with respect to any military action that we might take? And here I think we need to reflect on the notion of imminence, because everyone would agree that if you were about to be attacked and you could forestall that attack by acting first, it's entirely legitimate to do so—especially if the action you fear might entail weapons of mass destruction. . . . It's not that we're lawless. It's not that we're unilateralist. I would be the first to concede that we are having trouble getting others to support us on this venture. I think that's a great shame, and I think some of the countries that have refused to support us may not fully appreciate that one of the victims—if we in the end act with the backing

of only a small number of countries—one of the victims will be the very United Nations, the importance of which Chris invoked. Because if the UN can't live up to the challenge, if it falls to coalitions of the willing to do what the UN is unable to do, the UN will marginalise itself and demonstrate its irrelevance.[17]

Unilateralism

To Europeans, Perle's understanding of "multilateral" expressed here seemed highly idiosyncratic. He seemed to be suggesting that multilateralism occurs when others join in actions the U.S. leader has decided on—and if others choose not to join, then they are the ones who are not acting multilaterally and are consigning themselves to irrelevance.

Europeans, having been educated into the EU approach of inching forward collegially in policy discussions, were often taken aback as they encountered the American adversarial debating style, in which the best defense is a good offense. Quite a few administration officials and supporters joined Perle in denying that the solo abrogation or blocking of treaties was unilateral action—and took offense at the accusation. National Security Adviser Condoleezza Rice denied that the United States was acting unilaterally.[18] Under Secretary of State for Arms Control and International Security John Bolton denied it.[19]

Various commentators, seeking to coin the buzzword that would set the terms of debate, tried out different adjectives—à la carte unilateralism;[20] parallel unilateralism;[21] careless unilateralism;[22] gratuitous unilateralism;[23] and militant unilteralism[24] among them. Not to be outdone, *Washington Post* columnist Krauthammer coined the counterphrases "paralyzing multilateralism" and "new multilateralism," in which the United States no longer plays the "docile international citizen," but unashamedly pursues its own ends.[25]

Joining the linguistic and intellectual play, British and American (but not really continental European) academics fantasized that the United States might now found a liberal empire.[26] Unimpressed by the hairsplitting and fantasy, Patten urged the United States not to go into "unilateral overdrive."[27] But until the eve of the American-British invasion of Iraq, contrarian Tony Blair would continue to argue that while Washington talked unilaterally, it was acting multilaterally, and this was what counted.[28]

Given the sharp exchanges, how much of the American claim to world leadership did the Europeans accept after 9/11? Quite a lot, actually.[29] Certainly they accepted the fact that 9/11 changed the United States, and therefore the world, even if they did not comprehend the full depth of the shift in the American psyche. They understood that there was a totally new constellation, that the United States was not only a super-power, but a "hyperpower" (former French foreign minister Hubert Védrine) or, in irreverent Anglo-Saxon, a "superduper" power (former U.S. ambassador to Britain Ray Seitz). In the frequently cited comparison, not since the Roman Empire has any one government exercised such military, political, economic, and agenda-setting superiority over its contemporaries. And after the terrorist provocation it was obvious that the American administration and public regained the will to exercise this power, without the same aversion to casualties that inhibited them in the three-decade wake of the Vietnam War.

In the twenty-first century the corollary of this recognition is that either the United States leads in establishing the public good of the post-post-cold-war international order, or no one leads. Others may follow, or oppose, or try to modify U.S. policy, as Chirac has amply demonstrated. But no one else can lead. This corollary was grasped instantly by the British, Italian, and Spanish governments after 9/11, and it was a self-evident principle for the Germans as well, even if Chancellor Schröder would seriously misjudge Washington's tolerance for autonomous maneuver by client states within this overall scheme. It probably is fair to say that the axiom was even endorsed by the French, but that Schröder's misjudgment led France to lose its usual instinct for calibrating French exceptionalism[30]—or, less delicately, that Schröder's tactical move, made without forewarning of or consultation with the EU, gave Chirac all the excuse he needed to become the gladiator against the United States on Iraq.

All of the European political elites probably still agreed as well that if any nation were to have so much power, better the United States than Russia, Germany, France, or any conceivable alternative. And the horror of 9/11, with its implicit threat of similar violence in all open modern societies, only strengthened the Europeans' acceptance of hegemony by the one power capable of mounting a global hunt for terrorists.

The Europeans further accepted that the new threats of terrorism and WMD needed to be taken seriously and that international law would have to be modified to allow for effective defense against these dangers, just as international law had evolved in past centuries to let outside intervention stop piracy and the slave trade. Europeans were even prepared to revise definitions of preemption and the "imminence" that could justify preemption, though they would by no means approve as elastic a definition of these words as Perle was already using. Even the principle of preemption in the U.S. National Security Strategy that was being drafted for presentation in September alarmed European governments far less than it did the media. Rather than arguing abstract principles and terminology, professional civil servants expected to sort out differences in the interpretation of preemption pragmatically, case by case. Iraq, it appeared more and more, would give them their first opportunity to do so.

After years of prodding by Washington, European governments also agreed—this would be formally approved by alliance foreign ministers in Reykjavik in May 2002 and by heads of government in Prague in November—that NATO must help shoulder America's global security responsibilities and be able to operate outside Europe. "The defense of Germany begins in the Hindu Kush," was German defense minister Peter Struck's pithy aphorism for this shift.[31] And, of course, member nations had already authorized NATO to operate outside alliance territory on its own cognizance, without requiring UN Security Council sanction, in Kosovo in 1999.

Finally, Europeans agreed that Saddam Hussein was a monster to his own people, even if they did not see him as any imminent threat to themselves, to the Unites States, or to his neighborhood.

That said, there were major transatlantic differences about the proper application of the basic understandings, beginning with the style of hegemonial rule, as already discussed, the suitability of the military instrument to solve problems in the world, and the tension between unilateralism and multilateralism. "The American military is a terrific hammer. But not every problem is a nail," Europeans liked to say, quoting General Hugh Shelton, former chairman of the Joint Chiefs of Staff.[32]

Most fundamentally, perhaps, Patten and others dissented from the very notion that the war on terrorism—which is such a self-evident goal to Americans—can suffice as the organizing principle of U.S. foreign policy. Patten asked rhetorically if such a pessimistic mission, focused on nothing more than destroying actual and potential enemies, can really satisfy the optimistic American genius.[33] Others asked how a Manichean military campaign against terrorists and rogue states could avoid imperial overstretch and set sensible priorities to guide the commitment of limited resources in a world full of failed states. Within the United States, former national security adviser Zbigniew Brzezinski echoed the European skepticism about whether a war on terrorism made any sense intellectually, since terrorism is merely a tactic that can be used by extremists of any political persuasion. It is like saying, he mused, that America fought World War II to defeat blitzkrieg.[34]

Specifically, too, many Europeans were troubled by aspects of the Afghan campaign. Al Qaeda leader Osama bin Laden, "wanted, dead or alive," had slipped through the siege at Tora Bora, in part because the dearth of American troops on the ground left the task of capturing him to Pashtun troops of unpredictable loyalty. Bands of al Qaeda and Taliban forces were already beginning to regroup in the wild northwestern Pakistani border region. The Northern Alliance, representing the minority Tajiks in particular, was entrenched in all of the power ministries in Kabul, to the exclusion of the largest ethnic group, the Pashtuns. America's Operation Anaconda, which was taking place even as the U.S.-European polemics heated up in February 2002, was a disaster that left the U.S. army and marines (and the Royal Marines) exchanging bitter recriminations.[35] Most seriously, perhaps, the United States had vetoed in December 2001 the British proposal to give the International Security Assistance Forces (ISAF) responsibilities outside the capital as well as in Kabul, out of fear that ISAF soldiers elsewhere would interfere with continuing U.S. military operations. And the old warlords were not only beginning to fill the political vacuum again with a de facto partition of the country; they were being strengthened in their reconsolidation of power by the hefty American payments to local mercenaries and by the blind eye the Americans perforce cast on the renewed lucrative poppy growing. It was not exemplary nation building, and it threatened to undo the achievements of the dramatic military victory.[36]

Furthermore, hundreds of "enemy combatants" whom U.S .forces had captured in Afghanistan—including a dozen British and Australian citizens—were being held in legal limbo in the U.S. base at Guantanamo, Cuba. The U.S. government viewed this recourse as a middle way between submitting suspects to U.S. civil jurisprudence and treating them as outright prisoners of war, while still allowing humane detention in a situation that went beyond crime but fell short of declared war. Britain and Australia, concerned about issues of human rights, were urging Washington either to try or to free the prisoners, and they were backed by other European governments.[37] Yet it would be another year before closed military trials of the detainees would even begin.

For their part, quite a few Americans viewed the misgivings even of friends of the United States like Patten as nitpicking, at a time when the United States was facing a mortal threat, and as ingratitude for the decades in which the United States had provided security for Europe and relieved the Europeans of this responsibility and cost. In this view the European reaction was too little too late and deserved contempt. They found it outrageous that European allies could worry more about potential dangers in American power than they worried about the dangers of Saddam Hussein.[38] Writing in May, just after the NATO foreign ministers' meeting in Reykjavik that for the first time formally approved NATO missions outside Europe—the "globalization" of NATO the United States had long sought—Jeffrey Gedmin, the American director of the Aspen Institute, Berlin, criticized the "pathology" of Europe's aversion to the use of force. The security views on the two sides of the Atlantic were now so different, he said, that "the old Alliance holds little promise of figuring prominently in U.S. global strategic thinking." With the disappearance of the Soviet threat, Europeans no longer accepted U.S. leadership. Europe was "obsessed" with "multilateralism," "the code word for leveraging up the medium-sized EU and chaining down the mighty Americans."[39]

A few days later Charles Krauthammer too wrote an obituary for the alliance: "NATO is dead. . . . The proximal cause of NATO's death was victory in Afghanistan—a swift and crushing U.S. victory that made clear America's military dominance and Europe's consequent military irrelevance."[40]

Mars and Venus

As Americans and Europeans tried to discuss their differing perceptions, they seemed indeed to be coming from different planets and to be talking past each other. Americans accused Europeans of anti-Americanism and anti-Semitism. Europeans charged Americans with Euro-bashing and a wantonly pro-Israel bias.

Former speaker of the House of Representatives Newt Gingrich blamed the bad image of the United States on a "rise of a global anti-American network of activists and nations—including left-wing nongovernmental organizations, elite media, and most of the elite academics around the world (including in the United States)."[41] The reflex of anti-Americanism in Europe arises from an "envy complex," explained reporter Joel Mowbray of the *National Review*.[42] Indeed, anti-Americanism may have become a "permanent temptation of German politics," mused National Security Adviser Emeritus Henry Kissinger.[43]

Certainly a layer of anti-Americanism does exist in Europe. Novelist Günter Grass's views, shaped in the Vietnam War years, probably fit this category. So does Harold Pinter's blistering poem, "God Bless America."[44] British journalist John Lloyd scolds left "predestinarians" for seeing in the United States "an imperial predator whose actions—all actions—are conditioned by this aspect of its being."[45] There is the usual quota of warnings in France about American dangers (though perhaps an equal number of French books warning about the folly of America bashing). German newspapers regularly chastise those who caricature George Bush as a dumb cowboy who shoots from the hip. Austrian Green Party cofounder Peter Pilz condemns the "malevolent" American system as one in which the presidency is buyable, the media all say the same thing, civil rights have been suspended, and the two political parties only camouflage one-party rule with a plutocracy. Michael Moore's jeremiad, *Stupid White Men*, is on the *Der Spiegel* best-seller list, and almost a third of Germans under thirty believe that the U.S. government could have ordered the September 11 attacks itself.[46] The *Der Spiegel* and *Stern* weeklies cheered on German emancipation from the United States at the height of bitterness—though even *Der Spiegel* ridiculed the fast-selling book by "conspiracy freak" Andreas von Bülow blaming the original 9/11 attacks on the CIA.[47] For his part, Israeli author Dan Diner argued in his 2002 *Enemy Image of America* that there are deep currents of anti-Americanism in Germany in particular.[48]

However, Diner offers only one or two present-day examples in support of his thesis and uses the rest of his book to rehash the familiar story of antiliberal cultural conservatives in Germany from the Romantic era through 1945. Greek foreign minister George Papandreou says that much of what is called "anti-Americanism" is really "frustrated philo-Americanism."[49] Justin Vaisse, a visiting fellow at the Brookings Institution, calls Chirac "probably the less [sic] anti-American of all recent French presidents," and cites Pew polls released in June 2003 showing that anti-Americanism "has been receding in French society since the high points of the 1950s, 60s, and 70s." His conclusion is, "The French were against this particular war and anti-Bush, not anti-American."[50] Michael Mertes, a senior domestic adviser to Christian Democratic chancellor Helmut Kohl in the 1980s and 1990s, writes that a careful analysis of opinion polls shows anti-Americanism to be no more than a fringe manifestation in Germany.[51] And to an American who lived in Germany during the massive antimissile demonstrations in the 1980s, what was new about the brief German antiwar marches of 2003 was precisely the effort of protesters to differentiate between their opposition to the Iraq war and their affection for the United States. There seemed to be far less of what was widely parsed in the 1980s as a compulsion by German adolescents to break free from the American father figure. Moreover, the evidence of opinion polls sophisticated enough to distinguish between aversion to what America is and opposition to what America does in specific policies would also indicate that, apart from a low residual percentage of reflex hostility, European distaste for American policies in the past year or two can be taken at face value.[52] This begs the question, of course, of just when opposition to current U.S. policies might eventually accumulate to tip over into longer-term anti-Americanism.

In 2002–03 one complication that made it much harder to discern the real contours of European views of the United States was the new interweaving of the issues of anti-Americanism and anti-Semitism. The particular triggers were the series of attacks on synagogues in France in the spring and widespread European dismay at Israeli prime minister Ariel

Sharon's ruthless three-to-one reprisals for intifada bombings and continued expansion of Jewish settlements in the occupied West Bank.[53] Overwhelmingly, the desecration of synagogues in France was perpetrated by disaffected North African immigrants, but the acts were widely interpreted in American media as representing French and, by extension, wider European prejudices. Both tabloids and the quality media reported widely that a new wave of anti-Semitism was surging through Europe. "In Europe, it is not very safe to be a Jew," declared Charles Krauthammer. "What is odd is not the antisemitism of today but its relative absence during the past half century. That was the historical anomaly. Holocaust shame kept the demon corked. But now the atonement is past."[54]

In the *New York Times* Thomas Friedman speculated, "The anti-Semitism coming out of Europe today suggests that deep down some Europeans . . . want Mr. Sharon to commit a massacre against Palestinians . . . so that the Europeans can finally get the guilt of the Holocaust off their backs and be able to shout: 'Look at these Jews, they're worse than we were!'"[55]

More sarcastically, *National Review Online* editor Jonah Goldberg made the same point in putting down the French: "Even the phrase 'cheese-eating surrender monkeys' is used [to describe the French] as often as the French say 'screw the Jews.' Oops, sorry, that's a different popular French expression."[56] In Germany Natan Sznaider agreed about the resurgence of European anti-Semitism—but since anti-Semitism cannot be expressed openly in polite company nowadays, he wrote in *Die Zeit*, it has metastasized into anti-Americanism, which can be expressed openly. What better way to express dislike for Jews with impunity than to criticize the land that more than any other has given them refuge?[57]

Linda Grant disagreed, vehemently. As a British Jew, she said, she found the American Jewish conviction that there is deep anti-Semitism in Europe "preposterous, crude, xenophobic, hysterical."[58] Antony Lerman, executive director of the Institute for Jewish Policy Research in the 1990s, concurred, asserting, "The rise of antisemitism in Europe is exaggerated. Why? A mix of paranoia and a means of deflecting criticism from Israel. European Jews have never enjoyed such freedom and success."[59]

New York University professor Tony Judt used even stronger language to debunk the "Europhobic myth now widely disseminated in the United

States . . . that Europe is awash in anti-Semitism, that the ghosts of Europe's Judaeophobic past are risen again, . . . and that this atavistic prejudice . . . explains widespread European criticism of Israel, sympathy for the Arab world, and even support for Iraq." He challenged surveys the Anti-Defamation League was citing to prove that "'this new anti-Semitism is fueled by anti-Israel sentiment,'" contending that the ADL's own data did not show the correlation it claimed between domestic anti-Semitism and the widespread criticism of Israeli government actions in Europe. France's anti-Semitic Jean-Marie LePen is sympathetic to Israel, Judt noted, while Danes display the greatest pro-Palestinian sympathy but one of the lowest rates of anti-Semitism in Europe. Moreover, he continued, younger Europeans are much less tolerant of prejudice than their elders were.

What was most damaging for transatlantic relations, Judt found, was neither anti-Americanism nor anti-Semitism, but the "gap separating Europeans from Americans on the question of Israel and the Palestinians." In Europe, 72 percent supported establishment of a Palestinian state—the staple of all efforts to bring peace to the region—as against only 40 percent in the United States.[60] John Lloyd highlighted the same core argument: "Criticism of Israel is the central, neuralgic issue. It sets Americans against Europeans, because Americans—Americans as a whole, not Jewish Americans—are generally supportive of Israel's present policies towards the Palestinian *intifada* and Europeans as a whole are not."[61]

Whatever the deeper causes, the Americans gave back as good as they got—and then some. Any casual reader of the American press could be forgiven for picturing Europeans as the kind of wimps, appeasers, and ingrates who hold the Americans' coats while the Americans do the fighting, who take six-week holidays, live in theme parks, freeload on welfare boondoggles, fuss endlessly with their wet noodle of a European Union, and, in that ultimate sign of decadence, do not even breed enough to replace themselves. And then they kick the Americans in the shins. In the United States, "aggressive contempt" toward Europe prevails, "at least at the elite level," observed John Lloyd in the summer of 2002.[62] Richard Lambert, the former editor of the *Financial Times*, concurred, attributing the "deep distrust and icy contempt" of Europe in the American print media in recent years to the "right of the political spectrum" in the United

States. "For the Europeans, the hostility of some right-wing commentators in the United States comes as a real shock," he added.[63]

Comedians' gibes that the only way to get French troops to join the United States in Iraq would be to find truffles there were hardly surprising. But to have *The Simpsons* cartoon series invent an awkward epithet for the French of "cheese-eating surrender monkeys"—and have this name attain a certain vogue—was quite surprising. So was the anger at Europeans expressed by a number of senior American officials in background conversations.

By the eve of war in Iraq, *National Review* contributing editor Michael Ledeen would demonstrate just how hostile transatlantic relations could get by speculating, apparently seriously, that the Europeans might have been in collusion with the 9/11 terrorists: "Assume, for a moment, that the French and the Germans aren't thwarting us out of pique, but by design, long-term design." Cynical Europeans "dreaded the establishment of an American empire, and they sought for a way to bring it down." So they "struck a deal" and used "Arab and Islamic extremism and terrorism as the weapon of choice. . . . If this [theory] is correct, we will have to pursue the war against terror far beyond the boundaries of the Middle East, into the heart of Western Europe."[64]

In their own odd kind of way, the polemics demonstrated that there is a transatlantic political continuum after all. The Republican right berated the Europeans as proxies for the Democrats who were their real targets. The European left berated the Americans—who in fact were their real targets in a world governed by Washington. The name calling was all within the family. "But if a European writer were to describe 'the Jews' as 'matzo-eating surrender monkeys' would that be understood as humorous banter?" asked Garton Ash. "The emotional leitmotifs of anti-Americanism are resentment mingled with envy; those of anti-Europeanism are irritation mixed with contempt."[65]

Throughout the spring and summer of 2002 the American-European arguments droned on. In May the United States "unsigned" the treaty setting up an International Criminal Court that the United States had once helped sponsor but now saw as a potential trap for officers of the world's chief policeman. By threatening dramatically to pull all American peacekeepers out of the Balkans if immunity were not granted to every UN peacekeeper (including Americans), the United States got a one-year reprieve as the court came into being. That gave Washington time to pressure the new central European democracies in particular to sign bilateral pledges that they would never extradite Americans to the court; Romania and Israel were the first to sign up. In June the American president laid out the preemptive "Bush doctrine" at West Point, asserting, "The war on terror will not be won on the defensive," and "We must take the battle to the enemy, disrupt his plans, and confront the worst threats before they emerge."[66] Neoconservative calls for regime change in Iraq stressed more and more the Wilsonian theme of bringing democracy to Iraqis who would welcome their American liberators. The administration still had not fully made up its mind to oust Saddam Hussein by means of America's military hammer. But it was well on its way.

CHAPTER THREE

THE FRANCO-GERMAN-AMERICAN WAR

Fall 2002 to Spring 2003

IN THE LATE SUMMER of 2002, Iraq moved to center stage.

Europeans generally read Saddam Hussein's behavior as that of a quite rational tyrant whose drive to preserve power restrained him from launching WMD arbitrarily or getting close to jihadists who despised his secular regime. They thought that the containment effected by embargoes, no-fly-zones, and periodic bombardments by American and British planes had for a decade effectively deterred him from acquiring usable nuclear weapons or repeating the terrible chemical poison attacks he had unleashed in the 1980s on Iranian soldiers and Iraqi Kurd civilians. The one time when deterrence had failed, they noted, had been in 1990–91, when the United States had still been courting Iraq as a counterweight to Iran and when ambiguous American signals had let the Iraqi strongman think he could get away with seizing Kuwait. After the U.S.-led coalition pushed him back over the border, he remained contained for a decade, and they saw no reason why such deterrence could not continue to be effective. Nor were European intelligence agencies given any convincing evidence by their U.S. counterparts of a new threat of imminent Iraqi acquisition of nuclear weapons, attack on neighbors, or any direct link between Iraq and al Qaeda that might require near-term military blocking action.

They therefore saw no urgency in incurring the enormous risks of an invasion of Iraq in 2002 or 2003. Electronic intercepts and the considerable information gathered by UN weapons inspectors before Hussein's obstructionism forced them to quit the country in 1998 indicated that while Baghdad was in all likelihood trying to obtain nuclear weapons, it was still several years away from acquiring crucial materials—and that this gap could be maintained in the future. The general European assessment was that an invasion of Iraq might be the one thing that could provoke a cornered Hussein to a desperate third-time use of chemical weapons.

Moreover, many European governments held, an attack on Iraq could well lead to the breakup of this keystone Arab country, with Iran taking control of parts of the south and Turkey taking control of Kurdish territory to the north. Particularly if an invasion were conducted with the Israeli-Palestinian confrontation still at a boil, they reasoned, the result could be destabilization of the entire Mideast. They found eerie the increasingly voiced American expectation that democracy, welling up from Iraq's educated younger generation, would naturally succeed Hussein's tyranny in Iraq, bring the equivalent of the Enlightenment and the Protestant Reformation to medieval Arab Islamic societies, start a wave of modernization in the region, and promote Israeli-Palestinian peace. On the contrary, they suspected, any move toward greater popular participation risked empowering clerics of the majority Iraqi Shia, with echoes of the theocratic Shia rule in next-door Iran.[1] Moreover, with militants gaining in Pakistani elections, Europeans worried that an attack on Iraq could increase anti-American and antiwestern anger in the wider Islamic world, spread militancy among previously moderate Muslims in Southeast Asia, and perhaps even give fundamentalists access to Pakistani warheads that were not hypothetical future nuclear weapons, as in Iraq, but existing hardware. They feared as well polarization that could fulfill Huntington's prophecy of a clash of Islamic and Christian civilizations,[2] especially if Bush continued his uncritical support of Sharon's violent reprisals that were exacting three Palestinian eyes and teeth for every single Israeli eye and tooth.

The uniformed American military, the Central Intelligence Agency mainstream, and several foreign-policy stalwarts of the realist school from the administration of the senior President Bush seemed to share these concerns. In midsummer a series of opinion columns and leaks of military plans to the media raised circumspect but sharp questions about administration intentions in Iraq. Bush senior's secretary of state James Baker, National Security Council adviser Brent Scowcroft, and Gulf War commander General Norman Schwarzkopf were among the doubters; so was Bush's own Middle East envoy, General Anthony Zinni (who subsequently lost that post). Most bluntly, Zinni said,

> Attacking Iraq now will cause a lot of problems. . . . It might be interesting to wonder why all the generals see it the same way, and all those that never fired a shot in anger and [are] really hell-bent to go to war see it a different way. . . . The Middle East peace process, in my mind, has to be a higher priority. Winning the war on terrorism has to be a higher priority. . . . Our relationships in the region are in major disrepair [and] we need to quit making enemies we don't need to make enemies out of. . . . There's a deep chasm growing between that part of the world and our part of the world. And it's strange, about a month after 9/11, they were sympathetic and compassionate toward us.[3]

Cheney's Call to Arms

And then on August 26 Vice President Dick Cheney gave a tough speech calling for "preemptive action" in Iraq that instantly halted all op-ed what-ifs by centrist Republican, CIA, and U.S. military skeptics about a second Gulf war.

The key issue was not getting United Nations inspectors back into Iraq to locate WMD held in violation of a decade of UN prohibitions, Cheney said; what was necessary was to stop Iraq from acquiring nuclear weapons in the future by getting rid of Saddam Hussein's regime. "We realize that wars are never won on the defensive. We must take the battle to the enemy. We will take every step necessary to make sure our country is secure, and we will prevail." Saddam Hussein had ongoing biological and chemical weapons programs, and if he did acquire nuclear weapons, he "could then be expected to seek domination of the entire Middle East, take control of a great portion of the world's energy supplies, directly threaten America's friends throughout the region, and subject the United States or any other nation to nuclear blackmail. Simply stated, there is no doubt that Saddam Hussein now has weapons of mass destruction; there is no doubt that he is amassing them to use against our friends, against our allies, and against us." Therefore the United States would have to take preventive action.

With this clarion call, the "Bush doctrine" of "preemption," or preventive war, that would be a cornerstone of the forthcoming National Security Strategy took on concrete form. In an age when WMD might be acquired by terrorist martyrs whose fanaticism rendered them immune to deterrence by the threat of retaliatory death, Pentagon spokesmen stressed, it would be too late to wait for signs of an "imminent" threat that alone under existing international law could justify "preemption" of an adversary poised to attack. If the next terrorist strike without warning could kill not just 3,000, but 30,000 or 300,000 Americans at one blow, then the United States had to foreclose such a threat at an earlier stage, before terrorists ever got their hands on WMD. And the United States would be the sole judge of when that moment came.

"The debate in the administration is over. The time for action grows near. Congressional leaders should seriously consider a resolution authorizing use of force when they return next week," wrote *Weekly Standard* editor William Kristol in his introduction to the Cheney speech.[4]

Indeed, after initially maintaining that no congressional authorization for such use of force was necessary, the administration did seek congressional approval for possible presidential ordering of military action. It denounced any Democratic opposition to, or even hesitation about, military intervention as unpatriotic, a failure to act in the U.S. national interest, and tantamount to treason. In October Congress passed the desired resolution. Political Washington, including Democrats running in the November congressional elections, now basically united behind the course of war and threat of war. There was no robust policy debate in the United States for Europeans to join.[5]

Cheney's own hard line was, of course, no surprise. As defense secretary in the first Bush administration, he had commissioned the team of Wolfowitz, Libby (now the vice president's chief of staff), and other neoconservatives to write the 1992 "memorandum" foreshadowing a doctrine of preemption and unchallengeable American military power. And he himself was proud to be a hawk.

Nonetheless, confusion reigned in Europe about how to read the vice president's alarum. Despite Kristol's glee that the debate in the administration about invading Iraq was now over, Europeans were not at all sure that this was the case. The German government, for one, had been given

no advance notification of the speech and no guidance on how to interpret it, as would be the normal practice on a matter of war and peace.[6] It
would not be told until half a year later by U.S. officials that by then Bush
had already made the decision to go to war in Iraq weeks earlier.[7] It was
not yet public knowledge that the American softening-up bombing of
Iraqi fiber-optic communications cables to prepare for war had already
begun in June.[8] And European listeners had no feel for what the real balance of power might be within the conflicted Bush administration. Only
recently Kristol himself had highlighted the continuing differences when
he berated the Department of State as an "axis of appeasement" in its
reluctance to attack Iraq. Newt Gingrich—a member of the Defense Policy Board, a senior fellow at the American Enterprise Institute, and a
former Speaker of the House—was regularly trashing the Department of
State as well. Officially, the administration had not yet made up its mind
on war (and would not, officially, until days before U.S. troops cut through
the barbed wire on the Iraqi-Kuwait border seven months later). Yet how
could the American vice president be giving only a personal view on such
a grave matter? Or if his statement really reflected a policy decision, why
had the president himself not made the announcement?

At that point the weight and role of Cheney within the administration
was an enigma to European observers. The vice president had come into
office with the reputation of being the real intellectual power and shaper
of policy for the less experienced and less mature president. But no sooner
had this impression taken hold than some of the White House team worried that he might be upstaging the president. Thereafter, Cheney did not
seek the limelight. This new diffidence reflected reality, Bob Woodward
maintained; the vice president's role was "salute and follow orders."[9] Bush's
other early chronicler, David Frum, concurred, rejecting the notion that
Cheney was "a shadowy shogun who secretly controlled Bush, the weak
mikado."[10]

Others were not as persuaded of Cheney's modesty. Foreign affairs
columnist Jim Hoagland wrote about "a war cabinet of two—Bush and
Vice President Cheney."[11] Likewise, Zbigniew Brzezinski—an outsider in
having been national security adviser in a Democratic administration in
the long-ago era of Jimmy Carter, but still a savvy operator inside the
Beltway—contended that Cheney wields unprecedented power for a vice

president. He and his staff, Brzezinski said, constitute a parallel national security council inside the White House that fully rivals Condoleezza Rice's team and "is at least a coequal of the State Department in writing policies."[12]

After the Cheney speech a number of European observers began musing about the dark arts of neo-Kremlinology that were now needed to decipher American policy. It would not be until half a year later that a media consensus would form in Washington that the administration's "small group of war hawks" had created a fait accompli even before the Cheney speech by "persuading Mr. Bush to begin a huge troop buildup in the Gulf back in July—without consulting Congress or the country—[and] knew that it would create a situation where the U.S. could never back down without huge costs."[13] Richard Haass, in a valedictory interview as he left his post as head of the State Department Policy Planning Staff to become president of the Council on Foreign Relations in March 2003, would also date the decision time in retrospect as July of 2002—and confess that he had no idea how this rose to the top of the agenda.[14] And if an insider of Haass's rank could not trace the evolution, it was hardly to be expected that the outsider Europeans could do so. For them the old questions revived of how many Mideast regimes Washington might now decide, unilaterally, needed to be changed, and how long American patience would last during the long reconstruction period after such upheavals. The one sure conclusion Europeans could draw was that time had not, as they had hoped, cooled the ardor of administration hawks for invading Iraq.

The confusion in the European reception of Cheney's message was mirrored in the sequence of headlines in the *Frankfurter Allgemeine Zeitung* in the days after the vice president's speech: "Cheney calls Iraq a 'mortal threat'";[15] "The Union [German conservative opposition] too opposes any American go-it-alone";[16] "Government pulls back from promises of help to America";[17] "In case of an American attack, Berlin will withdraw its [bio-chemical] detection tanks [from Kuwait]," and "In German interests";[18] "Europeans: priority on diplomacy/different options," "Praise from Baghdad," and "Role-playing or conflict? Differences in the American government on Iraq policy";[19] "Schröder confirms his Iraq policy/America questions the closeness of relations";[20] and

"Schröder confirms unlimited solidarity," "Bush's man in Berlin isn't there for sweet talk," and "Religious war."[21]

The European Reaction

If the Cheney trumpet call to arms (as reinforced by the extraordinary Republican sweep of both houses of Congress in the November 2002 midterm elections) silenced American skeptics about intervention in Iraq, it did not silence European skeptics.

On the contrary, in Germany in particular, the vice president's words hit a raw nerve. From its inception in 1949, the Federal Republic had been trained, especially by the occupying Americans, not to glorify the military, but rather to eschew any resolution of disputes by force. So swiftly and thoroughly had West Germans internalized these lessons that founding father Konrad Adenauer already had to fight a major political battle to reconstitute a German army in the 1950s. Germans as a whole prided themselves on being a model "civilian power" and making a clear division between (moral) defense and (immoral) offense in the use of military force.[22] Without this metamorphosis in the German mentality, the Federal Republic would never have rehabilitated itself and achieved legitimacy in post-Nazi Europe in the eyes of its neighbors or its own citizens.

On the left, the conviction of the righteousness of nonviolence was only reinforced in the 1960s and 1970s as the American anti–Vietnam War movement spread to Europe. At that point the sense of German "kultur" as superior to the Anglo-Saxons' mere "civilization"—long a specialty of the German right—migrated left to shape a kind of moralistic anti-Americanism in rallies that continued into the anti-NATO missiles campaign of the 1980s.

Measured from here, the Federal Republic evolved with astonishing speed in the 1990s in its willingness to join allies in using force abroad. The first crack in the conviction of the superiority of peace over war under all circumstances appeared during the Gulf War of 1990–91. In the flurry of German and American media attention lavished at the time on white sheets hung out to protest against the American-led war and on the underground refuge granted to the two or three GIs who deserted from U.S. forces in Germany, the far more significant split in the left "milieu" in Germany went largely unreported. What caused the split was the dispute about whether or not the left's reflex championing of the Palestinian cause was covert anti-Semitism. When Iraq fired Scud missiles on Israel, it triggered pangs of conscience among Germans who had sought to do penance for the Holocaust by supporting Israel wholeheartedly in the years since 1949. For the first time in the "milieu," doubt was now cast on the absolute morality of opposing all wars; a competing moral mandate to defend Israel (and, as the Balkan wars raced out of control, to stop atrocities by local bullies there) challenged the two-decades-old certainties on the left.

Ironically, it was Schröder who pushed this shift the farthest. In his first four years in office, he performed a "Nixon in China" switch in military affairs. He had first made his name as a Young Socialist leader in the anti–Vietnam War days of the 1968 rebels. His Social Democratic Party (SPD) was vehemently antimilitary and sought to keep the creeping Bundeswehr engagement abroad in the 1990s at the lowest end of the spectrum of "Petersberg tasks" approved in 1992 as appropriate missions for any pooled EU forces—that is, peacekeeping rather than robust peacemaking. Yet with the Serbian massacre of thousands of Bosniak men and boys at Srebrenica in 1995 still fresh in memory, when Serbian strongman Slobodan Milosevic stepped up his bloody campaign to drive ethnic Albanians out of Kosovo in the first year of Schröder's government in 1998–99, Schröder and Green foreign minister Joschka Fischer persuaded their reluctant parties to vote for German military engagement in robust Kosovo peacekeeping—even without the authorization of a United Nations Security Council mandate. At a Green Party convention Fischer made an impassioned plea to hostile delegates, saying that for all of his political life he had had two principles: "no more war" and "no more Auschwitz." When these precepts conflicted, he declared, he had to choose "no more Auschwitz." He won the Greens' backing, with a narrow majority. The Bundeswehr took over a sector in southwestern Kosovo and quickly became favorites of Kosovar Albanians for their vigorous patrolling of streets, enforcement of curfews, and civil affairs construction.

Subsequently, Schröder and Fischer also committed German troops to United Nations peacekeeping operations in East Timor. And after 9/11 the chancellor even put his own office on the line in a touch-and-go vote of confidence in parliament to send German forces into combat, for the first time since World War II, alongside U.S. and British troops in eastern

Afghanistan. He sent the navy of the Federal Republic on its biggest deployment ever in May 2002 in command of the five-nation Horn of Africa fleet as part of Operation Enduring Freedom. The Germans further contributed substantially to the International Security Assistance Force in Kabul and took over co-command of the ISAF peacekeeping force in 2003. By then, finishing a remarkable turnaround that no observer would have believed possible a decade, or even a year, earlier, Germany had some ten thousand forces abroad. This was a number second only to the U.S. super-power—and constituted virtually all of Germany's much smaller deployable combat capability.

Iraq, however, was a war too far for the Germans. Some 71 percent of the public opposed it, as did even higher percentages throughout Europe.

As the metapolitical rhetoric about carrying out a democratic revolution in Iraq picked up in Washington, premonitions grew in Germany and more broadly throughout Europe. The talk conjured up personal memories of the carnage of World War II and historical memories of the terrible butchery of the Thirty Years' War of religion in seventeenth-century Europe and of Napoleon's "revolution in boots" in the nineteenth century. Many feared that the United States, feeling omnipotent, was now trying to play God in the Middle East. They would have been happier had they thought that all the talk about democratization in the Middle East was simply a clever spin on policies adopted for more cynical purposes (and therefore amenable to ordinary diplomatic negotiation and com-promise). Their contacts with Bush administration officials persuaded them, however, that their conversations reflected real motivations and therefore entered a lofty realm beyond the reach of mundane challenges based on mere cost-benefit calculations.

An uneasiness about the Bush administration's tendency to perceive its own policy as the dictum of Deity was first aroused among European leaders (except Blair) when they streamed through the White House after September 11 and were taken aback by the president's strong conviction that he was sent by God to lead the United States in its hour of need. These leaders feared that such certainty, combined with a Manichean per-ception of good and evil, could easily slip over into self-righteousness and permanent warfare.[23] Here it should be noted that much of the media coverage of this European concern has been misleading in reducing it to differences between godless Europeans and God-fearing Americans. Certainly in the case of Germany, quite a few leading politicians, including Christian Democratic and Christian Social Union MPs and Social Democratic president Johannes Rau, are no less devout Christians than President Bush. Religious conviction in Europe may incline in a quasi-pacifist direction that is just the opposite of contemporary U.S. political instincts, as the peace proclamations of Pope John Paul II, the Archbishop of Canterbury, and various European national Protestant hierarchies show, but these convictions too are firmly grounded in biblical ethics.

Compounding European queasiness was mistrust of the militancy of the American religious right, which enjoys more influence in the Bush administration than it has in any previous U.S. government. What Europeans tend to worry about most in looking at evangelical lobbies in Washington is the common cause they make with those Jewish lobbies that go beyond endorsing pro-Israel to advocating pro-Likud policies seeking a Greater Israel in Palestinian territories. Christian Zionists especially, from their literal reading of the Old Testament and the Apocalypse, strongly support a very large Greater Israel; yet all attempts to bring peace to the region over the past decade have depended on eventual establishment of a Palestinian state on those territories occupied by Israel since 1967.[24]

Even more serious in 2002—beyond any issue of specific religious fervor—was the European suspicion of the secular version of missionary zeal they saw in the vast social and political engineering project of democratizing the Muslim world that Bush was on the way to embracing as his own. Europeans viewed the West's victory in the twentieth-century cold war as the triumph of healthy liberal skepticism about all utopias over the contrary fascist and communist faith in social engineering. Now, however, Washington was asking them to take it on trust that this newest utopia of a U.S. grafting of democracy onto an alien political culture could really work. In Germany, the conservative and consistently pro-American *Frankfurter Allgemeine* newspaper called this vision "ahistorical" and "naive"; and the middle-of-the-road *Tagesspiegel* newspaper viewed it as a fantasy that could have been spun by Scheherazade in *Arabian Nights*. More circumspectly, the British *Financial Times* called it "heady stuff."[25]

The argument in these articles, which was representative of commentary in Britain and France, the former colonial powers in Mesopotamia (as well as of opinion in European countries with less experience in the region), was that democracy demands prerequisites that are glaringly absent so far in Iraq and the Arab world. Prominent among these are a strong civil society, a sense of individual autonomy, individual income that does not depend on the whims of the state hierarchy, and some sort of politics, however rudimentary, that goes beyond mere clan or personal loyalty to reflect interests. These preconditions did exist after World War II in Germany and even to a considerable extent in Japan, the two successful precedents of American nurturing of democracies that were being increasingly cited in the United States as models for modernization in American-occupied postwar Iraq.[26]

Europeans contended further that the Muslim countries that come closest to replicating these preconditions today are the non-Arab nations of Turkey and Iran—and that these two countries' difficulties show how unrealistic it is to expect Iraq to liberalize swiftly. Turkey has been democratizing for nearly a century, sometimes turbulently, and still has not finished the process sufficiently to qualify for EU membership. Young Iranians seem bent on loosening their country's theocratic rule—but are stifled by the conservative ayatollahs and their grip on military and paramilitary enforcers. In Iraq, however, Europeans anticipated that any real effort to plant democracy, especially by Christian occupiers, would only lead to electoral victories by the very Islamist extremists the United States was trying to defeat. The United States and any Iraqi government it sponsored would then soon face the unhappy choice of either empowering the West's enemies or repressing them.

More broadly, in the Gulf War a decade ago, the stated U.S. aim had been routine restoration of the status quo. This time, by contrast, the stated U.S. aim was shaping up as regime change, with its accompanying revolutionary secularization and modernization.

This vision of enforced change is far removed from the stability that was Washington's mantra under both Republicans and Democrats throughout the cold war and the first post–cold war decade; the latter is still the European instinct. The Europeans got their first shock over this radical departure when the prospect of a military attack on Iraq surfaced in conversations with U.S. officials in Washington shortly after September 11, 2001. At that time, according to a senior European diplomat, visiting

Europeans asked Deputy Secretary of Defense Paul Wolfowitz, the main advocate of military intervention in Iraq, about the regional destabilization that might follow, and worried that "many moderate [Arab] governments would be in jeopardy." Wolfowitz, the diplomat said, dismissed such cavils, asserting instead that chaos is a virtue and would lead to good results, since none of the governments in the region was really worth preserving anyway. His stance was so ideological, the diplomat indicated, that there was no way to discuss the issue rationally. Risks such as possible dismemberment of Iraq, civil war, elevation of Iran as the dominant residual regional power, a negative impact on the global war on terrorism, or negligence of the more imminent danger that terrorists might acquire nuclear weapons from North Korea or Pakistan all became irrelevant.

Given their belief that Bush's initial rebuff of Wolfowitz had settled the issue and their expectation that the hawks' passion for gambling on an invasion of Iraq would have to cool with time, the diplomats perhaps took Wolfowitz's campaign less seriously than they should have. But as Europeans—who are far more conservative than their American cousins—they regarded with foreboding any revolutionary policy of deliberately stirring up instability by waging a war that was only optional and not essential. When Cheney sounded his trumpet call in August 2002, they remembered Wolfowitz's words and took them very seriously indeed.

The German Elections

Germany's general election campaign had begun three weeks before the Cheney speech. This was an election that Chancellor Schröder seemed destined to lose. It set off what at times looked uncannily like a Greek tragedy that would end in the suicide of the half-century-old North Atlantic alliance. As so often in classical drama, the tragic flaw was hubris—the arrogance of power, compounded by the arrogance of weakness and the spleen that protagonists George W. Bush and Gerhard Schröder came to vent on each other.

All the well-rehearsed analytical differences—and they were real differences in mind-set between the United States and the European continent as a whole, and not just divergences between the United States and what Defense Secretary Rumsfeld would christen "old Europe"—

helped fuel the clash. But in late 2002 and early 2003 the driving force became psychological momentum.

During Bush's previous visit to Germany, in May 2002, Iraq had not been a major issue. There are differing accounts of the understanding the American president and the German chancellor reached then to keep the Iraq question from boiling up in the German campaign. Bush administration officials say Schröder promised to keep it out of the hustings; Germans say they were not primed by the Americans to expect any imminent decision about an invasion of Iraq that would require them to take a fixed position.[27]

This was the context in which Schröder made his fateful decision to pick up the antiwar theme on August 5. Germany would not participate in any "adventure" in Iraq, he told approving German crowds and approving European eavesdroppers, including a large number of backbenchers in Tony Blair's Labour Party. Nor would Berlin open its purse strings for reconstruction after the war as it had done during the first Gulf War. Nor, added campaign manager Franz Müntefering, would a Social Democratic government change its mind on this, even if there were a United Nations sanction for war—an inconsistent position for a German government that had always insisted on the legitimacy of the Security Council in such issues. As Schröder developed his campaign, he added a reference to a *sonderweg*, literally a neutral "special way," but historically a suspect middle way between East and West sought by Germany's cultural conservatives in their rejection of western liberalism in the late nineteenth and early twentieth centuries. In using the term, Schröder seemed to be talking about domestic rather than foreign policy, but the foreign-policy overtones added to Washington's suspicions.

Schröder's challenger, Edmund Stoiber, going the chancellor one better (until his colleagues pulled him back a day later), even said he would refuse to let the United States use Germany as its staging ground for any unilateral war on Iraq. He quickly retracted this position and thereafter concentrated on attacking Schröder for reducing the American pressure on pariah Saddam Hussein precisely at the time when the greatest possible pressure was needed to force him to allow UN inspections of WMD again.

With his uncompromising stance, Schröder left no flexibility for accommodation of either American or European allies on the issue—and therefore no room for coaxing a more multilateral approach to Iraq out of Washington by setting tactical conditions and then negotiating some in-between position. Domestically, however, his appeal mobilized two key audiences. The first consisted of those floating east German voters who had no firm attachment to any of the established (west) German parties, but were strongly antiwar—one of the few moral constants they could carry over from their life in the German Democratic Republic to the disorienting Federal Republic. The second was Schröder's own core network of SPD activists, whose "heart beat on the left," as the expression had it, and who had never before warmed to a leader they regarded as an unprincipled tactician for his lack of leftist zeal and his pitch to the center in his victorious first campaign. SPD Atlanticists in the mold of chancellors Helmut Schmidt and Willy Brandt were appalled. After a furious intraparty row, Atlanticist Hans-Ulrich Klose would lose his post as chairman of the Bundestag foreign relations committee.[28] Schröder would bar his foreign ministry from seeking any compromise position on an Iraq war at the United Nations and would flourish his new antiwar principle to win the support of approving party leftists for the liberalizing economic reforms they hated. In some ways the SPD, despite having reluctantly approved dispatch of the Bundeswehr to Kosovo and Afghanistan and the Horn of Africa at Schröder's behest, was now reverting to its more instinctive antiwar stance of the 1980s—and increasingly talking about "emancipation" from the United States.

Notably, despite popular German opposition to the approaching Iraq war, Schröder's *ohne mich* (without me) stand on the war set off no wave of popular anti-Americanism in the country. On the contrary, it elicited dismay from Germans who shrank from war, but did not want to sacrifice their friendship with the United States to the cause of averting war. In the quality press the chancellor was widely chastised for isolating Germany from its EU allies and especially—for the first time in the half-century existence of the Federal Republic—for alienating Germany from its longtime American patron. Criticism was only to be expected in the center-right *Frankfurter Allgemeine Zeitung* and the more right-of-center *Die Welt*, but it was equally vehement in the center-left *Süddeutsche Zeitung*.[29] And in regional elections in early 2003, the antiwar issue would find no resonance whatever as Social Democrats suffered their worst defeat in half a century.

To the Bush administration, Schröder's election foray was the first time in the existence of the Federal Republic that the head of government had run against the United States—and it was a personal betrayal of Schröder's promise to Bush. U.S. ambassador Daniel Coats promptly visited the chancellery in person to object to the antiwar appeal. And a flurry of op-ed columns appeared in the United States castigating anti-Americanism in Germany.

To the chancellor's entourage, by contrast, Schröder's position sounded no more inflammatory than the warnings being issued across the Atlantic by Baker, Scowcroft, and Zinni. And the highly unusual direct intervention of an American ambassador in a German election campaign seemed to be a throwback to the years before 1990, when West Germany had only partial sovereignty and the United States still exercised substantial occupation rights in Berlin. With no platform in America to defend himself, Schröder could only envy Senator Tom Daschle as the majority leader retorted angrily from the Senate chamber to Bush's simultaneous accusation that the Democrats were "not interested in the security of the American people."[30]

Bush was hardly swayed by the European sensitivities. But he did let himself be persuaded by the faithful Tony Blair and Secretary of State Colin Powell to give peaceful means—and the United Nations—one last chance. On September 12, ten days before the German election, Bush traveled to the East River to deliver an ultimatum. Either the Security Council would finally put teeth into its numerous resolutions in the preceding decade ordering Iraq to disarm or the United States would provide the teeth, on its own authority.

Three days before the September 22 election, the row between Schröder and Bush worsened. At a small rally German justice minister Herta Däubler-Gmelin called Bush's campaign for a war on Iraq an effort to divert American voters from domestic straits—and noted that Hitler too had used this ploy. While it might have been permissible for presidential campaign manager Karl Rove to muse that the adulation Bush was receiving from American baseball fans reminded him of Nazi adulation, it was definitely not permissible for a German to draw such an analogy.[31] Presidential spokesman Ari Fleischer called the comment "outrageous and insulting." The White House demanded that Schröder fire his justice minister immediately. The next day Schröder wrote Bush, saying there was no place in his cabinet for anyone who compared the American president to Hitler, but indicating that he would make this decision public only after he had clarified the matter—and after the election. Washington held this delay too against him. Eight months later, senior administration officials would still justify Bush's continued ostracism of Schröder by citing the chancellor's failure to get rid of Däubler-Gmelin within twenty-four hours—and his soft method of not reappointing her rather than firing her ruthlessly before the election. This incident, National Security Adviser Rice and Defense Secretary Rumsfeld both said, "poisoned" bilateral relations.

Two days before the German election the Bush administration issued its new National Security Strategy endorsing international cooperation but also enshrining unilateral preemptive war where necessary. It was proactive, in the analysis of cold-war historian John Lewis Gaddis; it equated terrorists and tyrants as sources of danger—and it risked slighting the tough job of routing out international terrorists to pursue easier and more glamorous wars on rogue states. Its argument was not that Saddam Hussein's Iraq was sponsoring al Qaeda, but rather that Middle Eastern authoritarian regimes, by their very nature, support terrorism indirectly in producing generation after generation of underemployed, unrepresented, and therefore radicalizable youths. The remedy would be to democratize these states and ensure observance of human rights, by force if necessary.

The National Security Strategy, Gaddis continued, shared Henry V's realization at Agincourt of the psychological value in victory "of defeating an adversary sufficiently thoroughly that you shatter the confidence of others." The strategy, however, also ran the risk common to Agincourts of inducing arrogance, including "the illusion that victory itself is enough and no follow-up is required."[32]

European foreign ministry reactions were more circumspect, and more pragmatic. Diplomats accepted the need for preventive military action on occasion in the twenty-first century. Indeed, Robert Cooper pointed out that the British government had followed this precept throughout the nineteenth century in determining when to intervene on the continent.[33]

In Germany on September 22 Schröder did manage to win reelection, with a razor-thin majority for his SPD-Green coalition. For the first time since German reunification in 1991, the Social Democrats performed well enough in east Germany to bury the Party of Democratic Socialism, the successor of the East German Communist party, which had outlived the German Democratic Republic by a decade. And the Social Democrats, along with the conservatives, proved once again that the extreme right has no appeal in federal German politics. Votes for antiforeigner parties were negligible; there was no German Jörg Haider, Jean-Marie Le Pen, Pim Fortuyn, or Christoph Blocher.

President Bush, continuing to take Schröder's no-war campaign as insubordination and a personal affront, pointedly did not send routine congratulations to the reelected chancellor and did not invite him to Washington. When the two leaders came together at their next international meeting, Bush turned his back on Schröder for all the TV cameras to record. Defense Secretary Donald Rumsfeld ostracized his German counterpart at NATO meetings; German diplomats in the United States were frozen out of contacts; even the normally welcome foreign minister, Joschka Fischer, on his first postelection trip to Washington, was barred from seeing anyone other than his protocol counterpart, Secretary of State Colin Powell. Senior Bush administration officials boycotted German (and subsequently French) receptions. Defense Department adviser Richard Perle publicly called on the just-elected Schröder to resign.

The frost was partly personal, partly a matter of policy, partly a reflection of the historical modesty still expected of Berlin, even if Germany was the most Americanized of all European nations. By all accounts, President Bush lays as much importance on personal loyalty in foreign as in domestic relations; after 9/11 all the wag-the-dog gibes that proliferated in President Bill Clinton's time were no longer tolerated—especially when they were overlaid with comparisons to Hitler. It was made absolutely clear to Berlin that, as one senior German official put it, while Bush considered Russian president Vladimir Putin a man he could trust, he deemed Chancellor Schröder a man he could not trust—and that this estrangement would not be healed as long as George W. Bush occupied the White House.

In this episode several further adjustments to the post–cold war realities of America's unprecedented military, economic, and agenda-setting supremacy converged. Structurally, the world's sole superpower asserted its unilateral right to determine its own military operations abroad. The

United States made it clear that it would select future partners in the global struggle to defend democracy not on the basis of shared democratic values and existing institutions, but on the basis of geography and the ability of others to contribute instrumentally to the achievement of U.S. aims.

And Washington amply demonstrated that it is the world's alpha male. Among other things, Bush administration officials saw their disciplining of Schröder as a useful object lesson for others. The episode had a salutary effect in encouraging rhetorical restraint in the contemporaneous Brazilian election campaign, they pointed out. If the United States could treat such a close ally as Germany so harshly, then lesser friends would understand that they must behave properly or risk worse punishment. The point was understood. A Canadian official who called Bush a "moron" was subsequently fired—and the BBC pulled a commercial that demeaned the American president.

European Worries

What got lost in the U.S.-German confrontation was both the actual extent of fundamental transatlantic agreement and the sober policy grounds for European resistance to war (as distinct from the no-blood-for-oil simplifications of the European peace demonstrations that were suddenly swelling to crowds of sizes not seen since the 1980s).[34] The point at which the two sides of the Atlantic did diverge sharply was on the least bad way to deal with the dangers. The world's sole superpower and policeman set out to nullify the threats. The more jaded Europeans deemed threats a fact of life that could be only coped with and managed, but never totally eliminated.

The can-do, optimistic, revolutionary Americans were further convinced that they could not only defeat the terrorist enemy militarily, but could even go on, as Wolfowitz had been preaching for a decade, to liberate Iraqis from Saddam Hussein. In a benign domino effect, under a short U.S. military occupation, democracy would take root and spread from Iraq to neighboring Arab countries. This in turn would cool Palestinian hotheads (and eliminate Saddam Hussein's blood payments to the families of suicide martyrs) and pave the way for an eventual Israeli-Palestinian settlement favorable to Tel Aviv. If it became necessary to use nuclear weapons to tame Iraq, some administration officials speculated, then so be it.[35]

By contrast, the status-quo Europeans thought it would be dangerous to launch an unpredictable war to oust Saddam Hussein, giving him nothing to lose if he fired chemical or biological weapons on Israel. Such a gamble in the combustible Mideast risked breaking up Iraq and unleashing civil war. Far better, they contended, to reinstate, under the American threat of war, the containment and inspections that in the 1990s had destroyed more illicit Iraqi weapons than had the precision-guided munitions of the Gulf War.

Moreover, should the United States go ahead and conquer Iraq, Europeans worried that Washington's habitually short attention span might well leave it to the Europeans to put out Mideast fires. The American public might rebel against the continuing deaths of servicemen in a far-off land—and the war's financial strains might tip the prolonged bear market into recession. If the United States then escaped its troubles by moving on to some more glamorous hotspot, this could leave the Europeans holding the bag in a destabilized Iraq. After all, Europeans recalled, the law of unintended consequences had already produced some nasty surprises in this part of the world. Washington's promotion of the secular Saddam Hussein in the 1980s against Iranian fundamentalists had helped consolidate a particularly brutal antiwestern dictatorship in Baghdad. And Washington's support for the anti-Soviet mujahidin in Afghanistan in the same period had midwifed the birth of al Qaeda.

Certainly there were ample signs of American impatience with the drawn-out process of institution building that would be needed to consolidate a peace. There was Condoleezza Rice's gibe about the Eighty-Second Airborne. And even Washington's follow-up financial pledges to assist in nation building to support the pro–United States government of Hamid Karzai in Afghanistan—the country that only a year earlier was the centerpiece of the U.S. war on terrorism—were forgotten altogether in the administration draft for the 2003 U.S. budget and had to be tucked in later.[36] In its first two years, the whole tenor of the Bush administration was that the globe's sole remaining superpower would do the war fighting of men and leave lesser cleanup tasks to the boys—such as the Europeans—who were too soft to join in combat.

To be sure, the Europeans were generally willing to take on this type of postwar role, in moderation. A German, Michael Steiner, headed the UN administration in Kosovo. A Briton, Paddy Ashdown, headed the equivalent international administration in Bosnia-Herzogovina, and the EU took over responsibility for training police there at the beginning of 2003. The EU would further relieve NATO of its light security obligations in Macedonia in April 2003, and French forces would shortly lead a European and South African expeditionary force outside the European continent in the war-torn Congo. The Europeans did not want to be stereotyped forever as the cleanup crews, however.

Most of all, continental Europeans worried—in this they were joined by Bush's staunch friend, British prime minister Tony Blair—that if the United States invaded an Arab country without first compelling Israeli prime minister Sharon to stop expanding Jewish settlements on occupied Palestinian territory and isolating Palestinian villages by building closed-off roads connecting the settlements, the attack would only further inflame Arabs and their fellow Muslims. Recruitment of suicide terrorists by al Qaeda and Palestinian rejectionists would soar. President Pervez Musharraf might be toppled by the many Pakistani fanatics; the madrasas might resume their preaching of hate; al Qaeda might obtain privileged access to Pakistani nuclear weapons. If so, an American invasion of Iraq might achieve precisely what Osama bin Laden had so far failed to achieve: uniting Muslims behind the jihadists, triggering al Qaeda's fervently longed-for clash of civilizations, and increasing rather than decreasing terrorist dangers.

At the end of the day, then, the question the Americans asked was: Is it better to get rid of Saddam Hussein now—or wait until he has acquired nuclear weapons that could kill millions? Their answer was "now." And the corollary question in pressing European allies for support in this enterprise was the old one posed to Pakistan in September 2001: Were they for or against the United States?

Conversely, the questions the Europeans asked were: Why is the wily Saddam Hussein more dangerous than the rash North Koreans, with their more advanced nuclear program and propensity to export missiles and weapons to the highest bidder? And would an invasion of Iraq fulfill the criteria of a just war in terms of proportionality, exhaustion of all nonviolent means, and probability of diminishing rather than augmenting evil? Their answer was "no." But in the public discourse they never managed to change the framework of debate and shift the burden of proof away from the issue of their loyalty to the hegemon to the issue of establishing a legitimate casus belli for this resort to war.

On November 8, after weeks of haggling, primarily between the United States and France, the Security Council finally passed Resolution 1441 threatening "serious consequences" if Iraq remained in "material breach" of earlier UN resolutions barring Iraq from obtaining or possessing WMD.[37] Hussein duly readmitted the international inspectors he had in effect forced out four years earlier. To maintain pressure on him to cooperate—or perhaps to prepare for coming war—the United States began a major buildup of an invasion force in the Gulf.

Berlin assured Washington that Germany, while not participating directly in any Iraq war (and not being asked to, as the United States kept stressing), would fulfill all its routine NATO commitments. It would allow U.S. flights in German airspace; participate in the international crews in airborne AWACS surveillance flights in the Turkish region; assign 2,600 Bundeswehr troops to guard American military installations in Germany, thus releasing American personnel for combat; loan Patriot antimissile systems and armored Fuchs biological and chemical weapons detectors and decontaminators to Israel; leave in place the Fuchs it already had on site in Kuwait; and send Patriots to Turkey by detouring them through the Netherlands (so that Dutch but not German crews would man them and thus formally fulfill Schröder's campaign pledge that Germany would not participate in the looming war). And it would shortly assume co-command of the ISAF forces patrolling Kabul.

As the Iraqi endgame began, the United States made efforts to repair some of the damage done to NATO. In late November the leaders of alliance nations met in Prague as planned, invited seven new central European democracies to become members, and approved two steps that were intended to restore NATO relevance in the twenty-first century. First—in a huge step for an alliance that for half a century had prided itself on being purely defensive and noninterventionist, a preserver of stability rather than a revolutionary—the summit formally endorsed out-of-area NATO missions in principle. Second, the summit approved a U.S. proposal to form an elite NATO reaction force (NRF) for swift deployment in Afghanistan-like crises. There was dispute about the paternity of the NRF idea. Some said American friends of NATO had invented it in a last-minute attempt to keep NATO alive in a way the neoconservatives might see as relevant; others said it was Rumsfeld's idea; still others said that friends of NATO had slipped the proposal into the policy mill in hopes that Rumsfeld would adopt it as his own.

On the other side of the Atlantic some Europeans initially suspected that the NRF might turn NATO into a kind of American foreign legion— or else a rival that would undermine the planned EU Rapid Reaction Force. Others took it at face value as a serious offer to give NATO a role in the unorthodox asymmetrical fight against terrorism and as a parallel effort that could even accelerate formation of the European Union's own intervention force through more robust standards and double hatting. Still others viewed it as the kind of two-edged offer that the Europeans could not refuse; if they wanted to keep the United States engaged in Europe in the sole institution that linked the two, then they had to agree or else be consigned by Washington to that constantly invoked limbo of irrelevance.[38]

Franco-German Relations

As 2003 opened, France again strode onstage, and the UN and NATO plot lines became disastrously intertwined. The humiliated Schröder, still relegated to pariah status by Bush four months after the election, and with nothing left to lose, reacted in the worst possible way.[39] He now tried to revive his fortunes by a quasi-Gaullist embrace of the French. The occasion was the gala celebration in January 2003 of the fortieth anniversary of the Elysée Treaty of post–World War II reconciliation between the two enemy nations.[40]

For the first time in a decade, Schröder was the demandeur in the bilateral relationship. Chirac seized the opportunity to prolong French grandeur and even, perhaps, to make good on what Charles de Gaulle had failed to do, by drawing the Germans into a tweak-the-Americans front. As the cold war had ended a decade earlier, France had been the demandeur. It had lost its status as an occupying power in Berlin as well as any political advantage from its nuclear force de frappe. Reunified Germany, by contrast, had just regained full sovereignty and a population larger than France's by twenty-four million, to give it even more weight in Europe. Just before the fall of the Berlin Wall in 1989, Germany had looked so dominant in Europe that Bush senior had seriously floated the idea of an American "partnership in leadership" with Germany. Furthermore, fifty years after the end of World War II, Germany no longer needed France's moral imprimatur to practice foreign policy; by then it was obvious that the old Parisian vision of France as Europe's political rider and Germany as its obedient economic horse was dead. France's one last advantage was its permanent seat on the UN Security Council, complete with veto. Now this veto and Schröder's misery in U.S.-imposed isolation gave Chirac a new chance. And Schröder's unexpectedly rigid antiwar stance left space for France to distance itself further from the United States, while perhaps still leaving leeway for rejoining the United States in the endgame on the usual French pattern. Indeed, Schröder's fear that Chirac would desert him at the last moment and leave him utterly isolated was a strong element in Paris's new-found leverage over Berlin.

The chancellor's lurch was uncharacteristic. Schröder had never before displayed much affinity for either the French in general or President Jacques Chirac in particular—a conservative who had blatantly favored Schröder's Bavarian challenger Edmund Stoiber in the September election. Indeed, for a German politician, Schröder had shown remarkably little interest at all in European Union affairs (or even in broader international affairs). German diplomats always braced themselves whenever their boss sat alone with the much suaver Chirac. Schröder had already been intimidated twice by "le bulldozer"—once in 1999 and again in 2002—into dropping the demand of his cash-strapped country to cut the extravagant EU farm subsidies that Germany essentially paid for and France essentially consumed. And now, in order to escape from his political isolation, he sacrificed three venerable principles of German foreign policy of the previous five decades.

The first and most obvious one was German insistence, ever since the 1963 bilateral clash over ratification of the Elysée Treaty, that no matter how important the French-German "alliance within the alliance" was, Germany's transatlantic relationship with the United States must always have precedence. The second was that Germany must not strike out on its own in foreign policy, but must always operate in multilateral forums; the unilateral stance that Schröder took in the electoral campaign and his categorical refusal to go along with any UN decision on Iraq violated this precept—and certainly did not match his constant badgering of his fellow Europeans to reach an internal consensus on foreign policy and then speak with one voice. The third, least noticed, principle, assiduously followed by his predecessor, Helmut Kohl, was Germany's longtime defense of the interests of the EU's smaller members (and in the 1990s of the new democracies to the east) and refusal to collude with Paris to establish a big-country "directorate" within the EU.

On Monday, January 20, France and Germany jointly initiated a debate about terrorism in the UN Security Council—and importuned Colin Powell to break the political engagements he had planned on the American holiday of Martin Luther King Day to join the discussion. When the American secretary of state arrived at the United Nations, however, he felt ambushed. Iraq was also on the agenda, and France and Germany were putting public brakes on any second UN resolution that would go beyond 1441 and sanctify the American drive to war; at a press conference French foreign minister Dominique de Villepin stated flatly that France would not approve any such resolution in the near future. This mattered; Bush's good friend Blair was facing a backbencher revolt against going to war without any more specific UN resolution.

Reaction in Washington

Powell was said to be furious. From that moment on, his interventions in the United Nations were as tough as those of Bush hard-liners. It could be that he had already decided in any case that the fait accompli of American deployment of so many forces to the Gulf by now meant there could be no turning back from war without enormous damage to U.S. credibility. And it could be that the administration had artfully planned beforehand the week of well-coordinated condemnations of faint-hearted allies that now poured out.

Whatever the real sequence of cause and effect, Washington certainly did erupt in anger. Defense Secretary Rumsfeld dismissed France and Germany as the "old Europe" and praised the "new Europe" of those countries that backed the United States, including the central European candidates for NATO and EU membership. As if on cue, Tony Blair, Spain's Jose Maria Aznar, and Italy's Silvio Berlusconi, along with the Portuguese, Danish, Polish, Hungarian, and Czech leaders, signed a joint op-ed piece in the *Wall Street Journal*. Under other circumstances the text of the op-ed would have been an unexceptionable statement of transatlantic solidarity, but in the context it endorsed the American march to war. This was followed shortly thereafter by a similar, but more explicit statement in support of the United States by the "Vilnius ten" central and southeast European candidates for NATO and EU accession. Despite all the pious professions over decades of a desire for a common EU foreign policy, both sets of signatories wrote their declarations behind the backs of their EU partners—and in their own defense charged France and Germany with having themselves launched a diplomatic initiative in the name of Europe without having consulted them.

This superpower cherry picking of central Europeans, who trusted only American, and not European, guarantees against any resurgent Russia (and were flattered by their sudden prominence), was devastating to the pretensions of EU unity. Especially in the 1990s, EU members had increasingly moved toward pooling their sovereignty in foreign as well as in economic policy. Reaching commonality had always been most difficult in the realm of external affairs, however, and now the recriminations over foreign policy threatened to erode even the hard-won commonality in economic and other domestic issues as well. Certainly they dashed Blair's hopes of bringing Britain into the European Monetary Union any time soon and of eventually establishing a healthy balance of French, German, and British leadership in the heterogeneous European Union. The acrimony threatened as well to complicate the EU's assimilation of the new central European democracies that Germany in particular had been nurturing for a decade—and to reawaken the long-standing French suspicion that EU enlargement would bring in a central European "Trojan horse" that would be more responsive to Washington than to Brussels. In a studied insult, Chirac said at a press conference that the central European nations had missed a good opportunity to shut up—and noted that the candidates might now have difficulty winning the necessary French legislative ratification of their entry into the European Union.

More ominously, the American coup raised the specter of a European slide back to the nineteenth-century balance of power of unstable ad hoc coalitions of the willing—the very Hobbesian all-against-all system the Europeans had striven so hard to escape from and replace after 1945.

Washington watched the European agony with *schadenfreude* and contrasted America's strength of will with Europe's balkanization and "appeasement." The armies of Estonia, Croatia, and Macedonia hardly gave the Americans the robust military help they repeatedly accused the old Europeans of failing to provide—but their solidarity did give Bush the political cover he needed at home. To an American public that supported an Iraq war only if the United States went into it with partners, the administration could and did argue that it now had eighteen courageous allies in Europe. "France and Germany do not speak for Europe," a bipartisan Sense of the Congress resolution proclaimed in lauding "the majority of Europe's democracies" that backed the U.S. countdown to war.

Transatlantic name calling escalated. Democratic congressman Tom Lantos, an immigrant to the United States and a survivor of the Holocaust, declared that the failure of France and Germany to "honor their [NATO] commitments is beneath contempt" and scored their "blind intransigence and utter ingratitude" for their rescue by Americans from Hitler and Stalin. Columnist George F. Will wrote that NATO is "a thing of ridicule" and wondered why any U.S. troops at all should remain "in an unsympathetic country such as Germany." American officials indeed speculated that when V Corps finished its job in Iraq, it might very well not return to German bases, but migrate instead to Romania or Poland, which have less finicky environmental restrictions—or even to the home constituencies of deserving American congressmen. For good measure, some Republicans called for a boycott of French wines and Perrier if the EU continued to block imports of American genetically modified foods. The Congress restaurant did replace French fries on the menu with "freedom fries." And in the most searing insult, Rumsfeld, momentarily forgetting the ten thousand German forces abroad in Afghanistan, the Balkans, the Horn of Africa, Kuwait, and elsewhere, delighted in telling a congressional committee that some countries were not helping the United States—like Cuba, Libya, and Germany.

Now it was the turn of the Germans—including those conservatives who had most bitterly criticized Schröder for damaging relations with the United States—to erupt in anger at this categorization. For his part, Schröder joined Chirac and, provocatively, Russia's Vladimir Putin in appealing for an open-ended extension of the UN inspectors' work in Iraq instead of an early resort to war.

At this point, in what was surely one of the most bizarre quarrels in the alliance's history, the venue of confrontation shifted to NATO. At issue was not NATO operational planning for the peacekeeping troops in Afghanistan that ISAF co-commander Germany wanted and the United States initially rejected. At issue instead, at the instigation of Washington, was formal authorization of advance NATO military planning to help Turkey defend itself in the event of war. This was something of a charade, since such contingency planning goes on all the time in any case, and various Turkish scenarios were in fact already under discussion, according to a senior NATO officer.[41]

Approval of this process by the political North Atlantic Council (NAC) of permanent ambassadors to the Brussels headquarters, however, became a test of wills. The United States wanted a visible NATO assurance to add to the multibillion dollars of economic assistance and other inducements Washington was offering to the skittish, just-elected moderate Islamic government in Ankara to persuade it to let U.S. troops use Turkish bases to invade Iraq, defying the 94 percent of Turks who opposed the war. The Turkish military command, otherwise Washington's best ally, sat on its hands, apparently because it wanted to see the suspect Islamic government take sole blame for this unpopular decision and, possibly, fall.

For his part, Schröder—while personally assuring Turkey that Germany would help it—wanted to demonstrate to the 71 percent of Germans who opposed the war that he could resist an automatic slide into combat.[42] France took the same tack. Belgium joined the other two in refusing to facilitate what under alliance rules had to be a unanimous vote, arguing that NATO must not preempt any decision by the UN Security Council on a second resolution on "serious consequences" in Iraq by prematurely presuming that ultimate resort to war. In response, Washington, which was happily pocketing each new German contribution while still refusing to rehabilitate Schröder, insisted that quiet guarantees would not suffice, that the chancellor who had defied Bush would have to make a public show of recanting by ostentatious support of Turkey in the war. More than one European regarded this as an attempt to force Germany in particular to become a little bit pregnant.

The standoff dragged on from mid-January to mid-February, when acceptable language about "defensive" aid for Turkey was found—and when a diplomatic compromise moved the locus of decision from the NAC to NATO's Defense Planning Committee, thereby excluding France, a political but not a military member of NATO. Along the way, the United States kept threatening that the alliance would be at an end if this issue were not resolved fast.[43]

Substantively, the specific NATO dispute may have been risible. But what was at stake was indeed the survival of the alliance. After fifty-four years of protecting Europe, introducing unprecedented confidence building in open shared military planning, socializing generations of American and German and Turkish and Greek officers to mutual trust, and helping the new post–cold war democracies to tame their armies, NATO now faced potential obsolescence, given American indifference verging on contempt.

For the Americans it was clear that Paris was the villain in gratuitously demolishing the transatlantic alliance. Some in Washington were so angry at the French—and at Tony Blair for getting them into the UN mess in the name of a spurious multilateralism—that they were ready to punish Europe by themselves helping to demolish NATO. For the French, the sparring may still have been a game, which they were winning on points. But to some Germans, Washington itself was the villain in sacrificing the alliance to its obsession with invading Iraq.[44] Their real worry was that the aggrieved United States might now declare its independence from an encumbering Europe. In the end only the hegemon that created the post–World War II cooperative institutions, in the belief that they magnified U.S. influence, had sufficient power to snuff out these institutions, in the belief that Washington was now strong enough to manage the globalized world on its own. "The prospect of war has divided the United Nations Security Council, riven the most enduring military alliance of modern times, and split the European Union," concluded the *Financial Times* on the eve of war.[45] America practiced "willful destruction of the international security system during the past few months," added the newspaper's columnist Philip Stephens a week into the Iraq war.[46]

At this point the UN inspectors in Iraq were still coming up with no more than inconclusive findings in their search for the weapons of mass destruction that the American and British governments said they knew existed. The inspectors kept begging Washington to share the intelligence that would help them find the illicit WMD. In early February Colin Powell made a presentation at the United Nations of as much proof as the United States said it could release, and the British government did the same in Westminster. The evidence quickly turned out to be seriously flawed in containing crude forgeries, plagiarism from a student thesis, misrepresentation of the purpose of some key cylinders purchased by the Iraqis, and exaggerated reports from Iraqi exile groups close to the Pentagon hawks.

On February 13 Chancellor Schröder told the Bundestag, "No *realpolitik* and no security doctrine should lead surreptitiously to our coming to regard war as a normal instrument of politics." On Valentine's Day an editorial in the *Süddeutsche Zeitung* stated, "The Iraq war is not legitimate self-defense. It is not humanitarian intervention. And it is not crisis control. . . . The war hollows out the international ban on violence; it leaves war to the whim of the stronger. The power of this negative model leads to geopolitical destruction; if it is legitimate for the US to conduct a preventive war, then it will be easy for other states to do so too."[47] By now close to 250,000 American and British troops were deployed in the Gulf area. On February 15 antiwar demonstrations were held in 350 cities around the world; an estimated three million people participated in Europe, with some of the largest turnouts in Britain, Italy, and Spain, whose governments backed the U.S. intervention in Iraq.

In the next three weeks the pace of events quickened. On March 1 the Turkish parliament voted narrowly against letting the United States use Turkish bases to invade northern Iraq;[48] American forces already in the country had to be redeployed to Kuwait or elsewhere to the south. On March 5 France, Germany, and Russia, which kept floating new proposals to extend the UN inspectors' mandate and postpone war, issued a joint statement saying they would not let any UN resolution pass "that would authorize the use of force." On March 7 the United States and Britain gave

Iraq a deadline to disarm or face war. On March 11 Defense Secretary Rumsfeld caused an uproar in Britain by saying that if Blair could not get a majority for the war, that did not matter, since the United States could handle the job in Iraq by itself anyway. On March 16 Bush, Blair, and Aznar met in the Azores for a prewar council. On March 18 Bush gave up on a second UN resolution. Tony Blair fought the fiercest battle of his political life thus far to get parliamentary approval to send a third of the British army to war without UN endorsement. He won, at the cost of the defection of a third of Labour MPs and the resignation of two top members of his government. Among western democracies, Westminster alone conducted a serious, substantive debate about going to war.

On March 19 the invasion of Iraq began. Unlike Bush senior's broad western-Arab coalition, this time around, 99 percent of the expeditionary force was American and British, give or take the odd Danish submarine and two hundred Polish soldiers. A "coalition of the bought," critics called it. Ironically, the Spanish fan of Bush contributed far less to support the war than did the German opponent of Bush. Prime Minister Aznar too had an antiwar public; no Spanish troops went to the theater or even backstopped the Americans.[49]

"The US administration visibly dominated by vice-president Richard Cheney and Donald Rumsfeld . . . scorns the multilateral at the core of Mr Blair's strategic vision," former British foreign secretary Robin Cook told parliament in an emotional speech as he resigned from Blair's cabinet. "The shredding of international support for America's stance over recent months has represented the biggest foreign policy defeat since the Vietnam War. Worse still, Messrs Cheney and Rumsfeld scarcely care. . . . We are back . . . to the Hobbesian world in which right is measured only by might."[50]

CHAPTER FOUR

POSTWAR EUROPE

EVEN WITHOUT ANY pincer of American ground troops from the north, Saddam Hussein was defeated in a swift, three-week march on Baghdad. What was billed in advance as a "shock and awe" campaign of over-whelming military power worked, if not in precisely the way planned. Night goggles and other Buck Rogers wizardry enabled the infantry and air support to fight not only in darkness, but also in the sandstorm that engulfed the troops early in the campaign. Hussein fired no chemical or biological weapons at the approaching armies or at Israel. There were no columns of refugees streaming into Turkey or Jordan. Unexpectedly, the Republican Guard did not put up stiff resistance, though unexpectedly the fedayeen did, before they were overwhelmed by American and British firepower. There was muted rejoicing, especially among Shiites, as tanks entered Baghdad and routed the hated Baathists, though nothing like the rapture in Kabul as boys could again fly kites, men could shave their beards, and girls with shining eyes could go to school to learn how to read.

The worst-case scenarios of the skeptics did not come to pass. American commandos got to the oilfields fast enough to prevent their being set ablaze en masse as in 1991. There was no nightmare of house-to-house fighting. The Turks did not seize Mosul, nor did Iranians seize Sulay-maniyah. The Arab street did not erupt, either in Cairo or in Islamabad. Intifada violence was no worse than usual.

Precision weapons worked as well as they had in Afghanistan, even in an urban environment (in which Iraqi forces chose not to make a stand). In fact, they worked better; in the clarity of the desert and in a real rather than a failed state there were no steep alpine valleys and murky loci of authority where one U.S.-allied warlord could easily slip the Americans "intelligence" that would loose satellite-guided JDAMs onto a wedding party of a rival warlord. Unfortunately, the search for the Iraqi president also worked just as well as in Afghanistan: Saddam Hussein vanished, just like Osama bin Laden before him. As of this writing, neither he nor any of his DNA remains had been found.

Initially, the victory in half the time it took to pacify Afghanistan produced the same kind of jubilation in the Pentagon that the Afghan operation had set off. America's lean twenty-first-century cavalry, defying conventional military dependence on mass, had prevailed again with speed and flexibility and net-centric gizmos.[1] Major combat was declared finished on May 1. U.S. forces could be moved out of Saudi Arabia and deployed instead to a suddenly friendlier Iraq—and not a moment too soon, as terrorist violence hit the Saudi kingdom too, killing twenty-nine in a western housing compound.

The downside was that now America owned Iraq, with a section of it sublet to Britain. And the new owner, with no experienced colonial service to draw on, did not know how to run the country. For Iraqis liberated from Saddam Hussein's oppression, freedom first took the form of unbridled looting of abandoned palaces and occupied hospitals, as American soldiers stood by passively. "Stuff happens," shrugged Rumsfeld. The American administration flirted with introducing an instant free-market economy, then on second thought did continue distributing food to the 60 percent of the population dependent on handouts. But for long months there was no restoration of reliable electricity or running water for city dwellers in the searing heat—nor were there jobs for demobilized soldiers, who took their grievance to the streets. The Eighty-Second Airborne was not in the business of escorting kindergartners to school, or ginning up the economy with workplaces, or policing the neighborhood.

Tanks on the streets of Baghdad turned out to be a clumsy and counterproductive way to maintain the civil order the population demanded. The American soldiers and reserves on the spot had neither the numbers of personnel nor the training to make good riot police. Mass roundups after the daily hit-and-run attacks angered innocents who got swept up. Reported murders multiplied thirty-fold in Baghdad. Rapes and abductions of women increased.[2] Nasty and just quirky rumors spread like wildfire. That the fatal explosion in a mosque had come from an American air-to-ground missile rather than a prematurely successful bomb-making class. That the soldiers' goggles enabled them to see Iraqi women naked by peeping through their clothes. That the GIs' body armor was air-conditioned, even as Iraqis sweltered. Convoys increasingly became the targets of snipers—and defeat of the scattered gunmen by provocative tanks in the urban jungle was an all-but-impossible mission. The deaths of American occupying troops after Bush declared the mission accomplished crept up to equal the number of battle deaths and continued climbing. The new U.S. Central Command chief, General John P. Abizaid, admitted that the United States was facing a guerrilla war. Iraqi policemen who resumed their old posts under American command also came to be targets of assassination, especially after audio tapes allegedly recorded by the live Saddam Hussein exhorted Iraqis to conduct a jihad against the "evil oppressors" in the country. Some 64 percent of the Iraqi population came to see the Americans as occupiers rather than liberators.[3] Many Iraqis who were originally hostile to Arab and other Islamist zealots who gravitated to Iraq to fight the Americans beginning in the spring of 2003 also came to welcome them after experiencing months of U.S. rule, according to Jessica Stern, an American academic specialist on the grim subject of terrorism. "America has taken a country that was not a terrorist threat and turned it into one," she concluded, and cited Saad al-Faqih, head of the Movement for Islamic Reform in Arabia in London, as calling the war "a gift to Osama bin Laden."[4]

Within weeks Washington fired its first administrator, a retired U.S. general, and brought in a retired U.S. diplomat, Paul Bremer, to take his place. Britain, which had cut its troops from forty-five thousand to sixteen thousand on the Tigris and Euphrates, had to bring back reinforcements; British public opinion, which had shifted from opposition to support of the boys in uniform once the fighting began, shifted back to disapproval of the campaign. Even the Americans started worrying about being overstretched in future crises as the time planned for occupation stretched from months to years and doubled in estimated costs to $4 billion a month. Half of the U.S. Army's combat strength was now tied down in Iraq. Concretely—and more to the point for Middle America—nine thousand troops in the Third Infantry Division had their return home deferred for the third time, and too many of the ninety thousand National Guard soldiers—the largest number mobilized for combat in half a century—were writing e-mails home about buddies who would be returning in body bags.

Owning Iraq meant owning its vast problems. And somehow all those young educated Iraqis yearning for liberal democracy did not reach the anticipated critical mass. By contrast, the clergy of the majority Shiites did have critical mass. They did an impressive job of keeping order among the million pilgrims who for the first time in twenty years were free to pour into Karbala and beat their chests in mourning for the martyrdom of Imam Hussein in the year 680. But the moderate émigré Shia cleric whom the Americans had hoped would help build consensus, Abdel Majid al-Khoi, was murdered on his first appearance in the land. The local clerics, while not imitating the Iranian ayatollahs in proclaiming a theocracy now that the Sunni Baathists were gone, were less accommodating; there were some fatwas against cooperating with the Americans. The interim Iraqi Council named by the United States in July to share the responsibility and the blame did so only ambivalently; the Council majority went not to locals, but to the exiles who had worked closely with the Pentagon in the previous decade. The politically adept UN special representative, Sergio Vieira de Mello, was blown up at the UN's Baghdad headquarters. Ayatollah Muhammad Bakir al-Hakim, a moderate Shiite cleric who was cooperating with the Council, was assassinated at his own mosque after Friday prayers.

Even worse for Tony Blair was the failure of crack American teams to unearth any more weapons of mass destruction in occupied Iraq than the disdained UN inspection teams had uncovered in Saddam Hussein's Iraq. Four months after the end of fighting, all that could be found were two trucks that U.S. Defense Intelligence Agency specialists identified as producers of hydrogen for balloons rather than mobile biological- or chemical-weapons labs—and some old plans for eventual resumption of a nuclear-weapons program that had been buried in the ground for a dozen years.[5] Gradually, various British and American intelligence officials who had felt misused by political leaders keen to paint as black a picture as possible of the Iraqi threat began leaking information about the forgeries, plagiarism, and hype that had gone into the politicians' public alarums in the buildup to war. The British government got into a nasty row with the BBC over one news report about political doctoring of raw intelligence—and the broadcaster won an initial opinion poll hands down, with 66 percent of the public trusting the BBC and only 16 percent trusting the government. More tragically, the bioweapons scientist at the heart of the dispute, David Kelly, apparently committed suicide under the pressure. For Blair, who had built his reputation on his own honesty and conscience—and who had built his case for the Iraq war on the WMD danger—the loss of credibility was devastating. For the first time in six years the Labour Party sagged below the Tories. By autumn, retrospective support for the Iraq war fell from 63 percent in March to 38 percent; half of British voters thought Blair should quit; and Labour's support dropped to 30 percent.[6]

In America the various anomalies did not at first bother a public that was still on a patriotic high. The made-for-Hollywood saga of the capture of Pfc. Jessica Lynch with her guns blazing, and of her snatch rescue from an Iraqi hospital, turned out to be just that, a Hollywood tale, but was laughed off as a bit of high-spirited public relations. Even the failure to uncover any WMD did not initially disturb the majority of the population that thought (wrongly) that Saddam Hussein had sponsored al Qaeda.[7] CIA director George Tenet took the public blame for Bush's incorrect assertion in the 2003 State of the Union address that Iraq had bought uranium yellowcake in Africa. The revelation in summer 2003 by retired ambassador Joseph C. Wilson IV that he had been commissioned by the CIA to investigate this claim and had thoroughly debunked it months before the president gave his address had little public impact. A prompt administration leak to conservative columnist Robert Novak that Wilson's wife, Valerie Plame, was a CIA operative—an apparent attempt to discredit Wilson's negative findings by suggesting that he owed his appointment to nepotism—also attracted little notice. George Bush looked like another Teflon president, on the pattern of his role model, Ronald Reagan.

Yet there were warning signs. Bush's popularity ratings were still high, at 60 percent, in mid-July of 2003, but that represented a swift drop of nine points in less than three weeks.[8] Half of the American public thought President Bush had exaggerated the Iraqi nuclear threat.[9] New American Army Chief of Staff Peter J. Schoomaker told Congress that the army would probably have to be enlarged to meet worldwide U.S. commitments.[10] And for the first time a majority of voters told pollsters that they found the continuing casualties in Iraq unacceptable.

By then, al Qaeda and the Taliban were reestablishing themselves in the Afghan-Pakistan border area, and al Qaeda was expanding its links with diverse local terrorists across Southeast Asia.[11] Western intelligence reports said the number of Islamist terrorist recruits was increasing following the Iraq war. In much of the Arab world Osama was the favorite name for baby boys.

Differing Questions

After the war there were three major questions for the Europeans: how to defuse tensions in the Middle East; how to heal the transatlantic rupture; and how to heal the intra-European rupture. All three were inextricably intertwined. A fourth question—this was at first a matter for quiet high-level soundings rather than public pronouncements—was how to move toward an acknowledgment in principle that Europe shared America's fears about terrorism and WMD, even if not always America's choice of defense against them. A fifth question still waited in the wings—how to pay for procurement of military capacities that might possibly get Washington to take Europeans more seriously.[12]

America's postwar questions were different. The operative priority was on leveraging the country's first successful preemptive war into pressure on Syria, on would-be nuclear Iran—and, if possible, on North Korea, which, according to reports, already possessed enough plutonium to make its first nuclear bombs. The broader policy question was how to effect the revolutionary transformation of dangerous despots in the Middle East as a whole to reduce the combustibility of the region. As Thomas Donnelly put it in the American Enterprise Institute's online National Security Outlook:

The Bush Doctrine proposes that the United States foster the spread of classical liberalism—its institutions and values—in order to undermine dictatorships ruled by terror and ultimately to replace them with just, representative societies. The real question now is how the United States can leverage its victory in Iraq to uphold, expand, and institutionalize the Pax Americana.... The Bush Doctrine amounts to "rolling back" radical Islamism while "containing" the People's Republic of China, that is, hedging against its rise to great-power status.[13]

In Washington's hierarchy of concerns, repair of relations with Europe ranked low. It was assumed that the swift U.S. military triumph in Iraq would show the Europeans that they had been wrong to be so timorous about the war—and that the mass graves of Saddam Hussein's victims would convince observers that far fewer Iraqis died in the war than would have died had Hussein continued his rule of terror.[14] And anyway, even if they did not admit the error of their ways, the Europeans would now have to adjust to the world as America had remade it. The United States was not looking for love; it was looking for respect.[15] Its willingness to exercise power would ensure maximum European loyalty. And a little skillful U.S. maneuvering—perhaps by "disaggregating" other EU members from pernicious French-German leadership, on the lines of the *Wall Street Journal* 8 and the Vilnius 10 could help speed the process.[16] The proper way to deal with European malcontents, in the maxim attributed to Condoleezza Rice, was to forgive the Russians, ignore the Germans, and punish the French. In line with this precept, German and French firms were discouraged from applying for subcontracts in Iraqi reconstruction (they were already barred from primary U.S. contracts by Congress) by such means as not inviting them to meetings giving initial data about the jobs to be let.[17]

The rather different answers to the main questions posed by the Europeans were first articulated by new European Tony Blair on the eve of the Iraq war, and were valid for new and old Europeans alike. The aims were to persuade George Bush to become actively engaged in the search for an Israeli-Palestinian peace settlement; to trade off full European participation in postwar Iraqi reconstruction for U.S. acceptance of UN supervision of the job; and to use these common causes to rebuild U.S.-European amity.[18] A European Union summit that assembled days after the war started set aside intramural feuds to back these aims and call unanimously for the UN to have "a central role during and after the current crisis." The summit declaration further asked for a relaunch of the Israeli-Palestinian peace process after two years of violence to realize the "vision of two States living side by side in peace and security." It urged the United States to help by permitting publication of the U.S.-European-Russian-UN "road map" to this goal drawn up the previous December on a European draft by the "Quartet" of the United States, the EU, the UN, and Russia.[19]

While discreetly making clear that this time they would not offset the bulk of Washington's war costs, as they and Japan did together in 1991, Germany, France, and the EU all signaled their readiness to contribute to postwar humanitarian aid and, if there were a UN mandate in Iraq, nation building.[20] Significantly, the EU summit commissioned Solana to draft the EU's first-ever strategy statement laying out threats and measures to defend against them, as perceived by the Europeans.

Tony Blair, invited to run a victory lap in Washington by addressing an unusual joint session of Congress in mid-July, did not again call there for greater internationalization of the postwar effort to stabilize Iraq. Instead, he focused on the desideratum of a just Israeli-Palestinian settlement.[21]

Continental Europeans were less sanguine about prospects than was the ever optimistic Blair, who seemed convinced that he could bring skeptics on both sides of the Atlantic around to his grand reconciliation project. What hope the continentals did have for improving relations with the United States was vested instead in a development they half desired, half dreaded—a return of checks and balances to the monopolitical American landscape as a result of growing American disillusionment with the onerous imperial tasks in Iraq. On the one hand, European officials fervently wished for maximum American success in Iraq; failure could leave the Middle East more dangerous than ever, and any new Vietnam syndrome, even short of an abrupt U.S. pullout, would be disastrous. On the other hand, too much American success, as in the initial months in Afghanistan, might only stoke American ardor for military intervention in Syria or in axis-of-evil Iran.

In the case of Iran, Europeans, seeing the country as the one Islamic nation in the region that did have a critical mass of young people longing for modernization, thought the best way for the West to support student demonstrators and the reforming President Mohammad Khatami was a "critical dialogue" with Tehran to encourage both domestic relaxation and acceptance of international nuclear inspections. The Americans, by contrast, despite welcoming Iran's anti-Taliban position in the fall of 2001, had given up on Khatami as ineffectual and were again talking of the need for radical regime change in Tehran. In the American view, the Europeans were putting far too much credence in dialogue and far too little muscle behind criticism of Iran's apparent effort to build nuclear weapons under cover of its nuclear energy program. Pentagon officials and their think-tank allies stated that regime change did not necessarily mean war with Iran; but they implied strongly that a failure of Iran to change the regime on its own (or to renounce all suspect nuclear activity) could make war a real option. For the time being, though, Americans saw their Iraq-induced pressure on Syria and Iran as working. Damascus seemed to be pulling back from cross-border support of Baathists in Iraq, while Iran was pulling back from blatant meddling in Iraqi postwar politics.

Relaunching the Peace Process

As Bush traveled to Europe at the end of May for the gala three hundredth anniversary of St. Petersburg and the G-8 summit in Evian, he had finally reengaged personally, to the gratification of the Europeans, in the search for Israeli-Palestinian peace. This echoed the move his father had made after the Gulf War in getting the Israeli and Palestinian adversaries to relaunch in Madrid a "peace process" that came closer to success than any previous attempt at a land-for-peace deal. It was a major shift for George W. Bush, who (apart from one abortive statement about a two-state solution in summer of 2002) had essentially backed Prime Minister Ariel Sharon's tough military response to the intifada unquestioningly, apparently in consonance with his own political and religious beliefs.[22] Now, immediately after the G-8 meeting, he would fly to meet Israeli prime minister Sharon and new Palestinian Council prime minister Mahmoud Abbas at Aqaba, where his two interlocutors would at last pledge to implement the Quartet's road map. As a first step, Sharon would accept the goal of a Palestinian state, begin tearing down unapproved settler outposts on occupied territory earmarked for that state, and hand Bethlehem back to control by the Palestinian Authority. Abbas would call for an end to Palestinian suicide attacks on Israelis, and Hamas and Islamic Jihad, the two most militant groups, would agree to a "truce."

The new U.S. engagement in the Mideast eased transatlantic strains. Europeans were unsure, though, if Bush's resolve would outlast the beginning of the president's reelection campaign in 2004. And despite the Quartet's agreement on the generalities of the road map, they knew that the history of transatlantic quarrels over the Mideast boded ill for U.S.-European consonance through the inevitable crises in the three-year eternity projected for implementing the road map. In the 1940s and 1950s Washington and London had fought over creation of the state of Israel, relations with Mossadeq's Iran, and, of course, Suez. The United States and Europe had quarreled over the 1973 Israeli-Arab war and the oil crisis, then over the Iranian hostage crisis in the 1980s. The United States and Germany had clashed over the 1991 Gulf War and subsequent Anglo-American air raids in Iraq.[23] Repeatedly, Israel had been a bone of contention as France in particular pursued a strongly pro-Arab course in the 1970s and 1980s. And dissonance between France and other Europeans over Mideast issues had been a major prod to the European Community to begin harmonizing foreign policy in "European Political Cooperation" in the 1970s.

Over decades, EPC and a mellowing of France's stark pro-Arab stance did bring some convergence in European policies. In the 1990s the Europeans backed the Oslo process, which continued what had been started at Madrid. The EU also covered administrative expenses of the experimental alternative to violence of the semiautonomous Palestinian Authority—and thus relieved Israel of the costs of caring for populations in occupied territories required by international law.

As the second intifada stepped up violence in 2000 and 2001, the Europeans shifted their policy on the Palestinian Authority in two ways. They stopped some funding for civil administration that they suspected might be going instead to private or terrorist pockets, and they finally accepted the political bankruptcy of Palestinian Council president Yasir Arafat.

High Representative Solana worked together with Americans in negotiating with and putting pressure on Arafat to cede authority to a new and more pragmatic prime minister, Mahmoud Abbas.[24] German foreign minister Joschka Fischer, who took a keen personal interest in these issues and won unusual trust from the Israeli as well as from the Palestinian side, was also able to offer his tactical good offices at one point to help resolve a standoff between Israeli soldiers and Palestinian gunmen barricaded inside a Christian church.

This by no means added up to European activism in Israel independent of the United States. While Europeans differed from the United States in deeming Sharon's use of force excessive, they understood that only Israel's political and financial superpower patron could ever nudge Sharon to compromises—and only this superpower had sufficient raw power and influence with both sides to act as a broker between the two. The Europeans' chief hope, therefore, was that Bush would persevere in pursuing the road map, despite the predictable sabotage of negotiations by Palestinian and Israeli extremists. As the peace process once again broke down, violence resumed, and Abbas was forced out of office after only a few months. However, Europeans by and large returned to their original assumption that Bush would always back Israeli hard-liners. There was no more than symbolic dismantlement of outposts on occupied territory, and Sharon proceeded with building a Chinese wall to protect the scattered Israeli settlements in a way that separated still more Palestinians from their fields and their relatives. A common view was that Sharon treated Bush with "open contempt."[25] "It isn't a Quartet," complained a senior EU official involved in Mideast diplomacy with the UN, Russia, and the United States. "It's three against one."[26]

As President Bush prepared his keynote speech in Krakow on his first postwar visit to Europe in June, Europeans hoped that he would make some gesture of conciliation to them—and senior U.S. officials insisted in talks with journalists that he did so. "Old" Europeans read Bush's words there rather differently, however. The president did not mention the European Union once, despite the crucial Polish referendum on joining the EU that was coming up in a few days. He also praised Poland's long-standing ties to America in a way that smacked more of disaggregation than of the fifty-year-old U.S. policy of encouraging progressive European integration.

Halving the regular American-EU summits from a biannual to an annual rhythm, as Bush did, was one thing; goading the largest new entrant to the EU to fulfill French fears that it would be an American agent in the EU was quite another. "Poland is a good citizen of Europe and Poland is a close friend of America—and there is no conflict between the two," declared Bush, with the ease of the victor assuring the vanquished in a fraught triangle that the lady would still be good friends with him too. "This is a time for all of us to unite in the defense of liberty and to step up to the shared duties of free nations. This is no time to stir up divisions in a great alliance."[27] Implicit was the reproach to any old Europeans who might try to block new Europeans, for example, from yielding to Washington's renewed campaign to get others to sign bilateral exemptions for American citizens from the jurisdiction of the new International Criminal Court—or else have U.S. military aid retracted.

Implicit too was a smirk about America's surprise coup in awarding fledgling NATO member Poland the command of a third multinational sector in Iraq, to join the American and British sectors and be manned by 9,200 Ukrainian, Spanish, Bulgarian, Romanian, Hungarian, South American, and Polish troops. To fulfill the task, Warsaw—which had contributed two hundred GROM special forces to the Iraq war—would need both full U.S. bankrolling of its command and full NATO support (already granted) in communications, transport, and intelligence. The recalcitrant Germans and French were thus clearly put on notice that if their price for participating in Iraqi reconstruction was service under UN political stewardship rather than solo American military occupation, then Washington could do without them.[28]

The Poles, with their long ties with "Polonia" émigrés in the United States and a romantic nineteenth-century view of military exploits untainted by Germany's twentieth-century revulsion against war, were flattered by the honor. And they stoutly denied that they were in any way betraying Berlin's special mentoring of them for EU membership in the 1990s against the opposition of all other EU members except Britain.[29] The Poles still hedged their American allegiance, however; when referendum day came, Polonia in Chicago may have voted against EU membership, but Polonia elsewhere in the United States voted with the overwhelming majority in the home country to approve accession. Significantly, so did the Polish Catholic church, in a move that presaged greater future identification with the European Union. Despite its earlier fears that the EU would bring pornography, divorce, and de-Christianization to Poland, the church hierarchy told parishioners to vote in the referendum in sufficient numbers to validate the result—and Pope John Paul II even told them to vote yes. Furthermore, as the initial euphoria of playing in the big leagues wore off, the Polish public became more ambivalent about Warsaw's role in Iraq.[30]

As President Bush moved on from Krakow to St. Petersburg, the big news was that he stopped by Gerhard Schröder's dinner table to ask, "How are you?" and the chancellor managed to reply, "Fine," before Bush stepped away again.[31] But eight months after the German election, it was still too early for any bilateral rapprochement.

Nor was it yet time for the White House to stop punishing G-8 host Chirac, whom Bush talked with at Evian no longer than protocol required. France was continuing to defy the United States and had only recently led Germany, Belgium, and the martial giant of Luxembourg into a minisummit in Brussels to declare a core European "defense union." Paris clearly wanted this avant-garde to become a rival to NATO and help shape a multipolar rather than unipolar world—even if Berlin hoped, obversely, to gain political cover for some modest increases in defense outlays to bolster the European contribution to NATO. Germany had backpedaled away from French visions all the way to the summit and cleared communiqué language with the British at every point. In the end, the only concrete element objectionable to NATO had ended up being establishment of an autonomous planning staff that was too tiny to do much harm.[32] But the "praline summit," as it was sardonically called, rankled Americans. "Now the people who thought we could go back to business as usual [with Europe] were proved wrong. We can't consider the disagreement over Iraq an aberration," one unnamed senior American official told the *Wall Street Journal* after the minisummit. The *Journal* editor noted, "The truth is that American conservatism, which is heavily represented in the Bush administration, is itself split between those who think NATO is a touchstone and those who think, well, good-riddance to the Europeans."[33] NATO secretary-general Lord Robertson felt obliged to assert, "The Atlantic Alliance—NATO—is neither broken nor marginalized," and to dismiss alliance rows as unfortunate, but no more than a "hit above the waterline."[34]

In mid-June Solana presented to European leaders the draft strategy paper he had been commissioned to write as a basis for their discussion, modification, and final adoption at the end of 2003. Europe's first joint security strategy had to bridge not only transatlantic gaps, but also differences between the eleven EU members who also belonged to NATO and the four neutral EU states of Austria, Sweden, Finland, and Ireland. The paper went much further than any previous EU statement in accepting America's post–9/11 threat assessment and identified the interaction between terrorism, proliferation of WMD, failed states, and organized crime as a grave danger. It urged the Europeans to counter the threats, first, by extending their immediate zone of security into what is sometimes called, with a bow to Soviet coinage of the phrase, the EU's "near abroad." That would entail finding ways to apply to noncandidates Russia and Ukraine the transforming and stabilizing effect the EC/EU had on post-dictatorship Spain and Portugal in the 1970s and is now having on the central European, Turkish, and Balkan candidates for EU membership.

That part of the paper was not altogether new. Nor was the general call for multilateralism and respect for international law. Nor was the summons to improve European capabilities through more defense spending, more pooling of resources, and more detailed intelligence coordination of continuing threat assessments.

What was very new was the draft's endorsement of preventive action. The main emphasis was on Europe's trademark humanitarian and development aid, political counseling, and other peaceful tools of crisis prevention. Given the risks of megadeaths in the combination of terrorism and WMD, however, allowance was also made in extraordinary cases for preemptive military action of the sort enshrined in the American National Security Strategy.[35]

This statement, the Europeans believed, was an invitation to Washington to leapfrog the dissension over the Iraq war and open a fresh transatlantic security dialogue on the basis of greater post-Iraq sobriety all around. The paper did not suggest correctives for the unhappy de facto division of labor today, in which "the US does the fighting, the UN feeds, the EU pays," or, in the shorter variant, "The US does dinner, and the EU does the dishes." But European officials were already wrestling with this problem in planning the outfitting and training of the NATO and EU rapid reaction forces and any more serious involvement of NATO in ensuring security in postwar Iraq. In April NATO had already agreed for the first time to assume command of an out-of-Europe operation, in Afghanistan—a step the Germans had long desired and the United States had at first rejected, but later agreed to. As disillusionment with a long U.S. stay in Iraq spread in America and Congress sought NATO engagement to help lighten the burden, the preconditions seemed to exist for some kind of compromise that could expand the UN's political role in the country and thus enable French and German NATO troops (and Indians, Japanese, and others) to participate.

Looking Ahead

This account of the near-death of the transatlantic alliance in 2003 closes in medias res. That part of the security relationship institutionalized in NATO has suffered a severe hit from friendly fire, but, in the end, the damage may have been kept above the water line, as Lord Robertson asserted. That part of the security relationship institutionalized in the European Union has also been dealt a severe blow, and it will take another year at least to see whether this hit was sustained aboveboard or in the hull. Finally, the alliance's uninstitutionalized core of trust too has been violated. That may be the hardest to restore.

In all three areas the outcome will depend on the reaction of the principals. Near-death experiences are said to transform survivors. This particular one may do so too—but for now the process of transformation poses far more questions than it answers.

In the case of the world's longest-lasting military alliance, survival of the battered North Atlantic Treaty Organization in 2003 depended on its assumption, sight unseen, of a global role for the first time in its history. It agreed to its first out-of-Europe mission in taking on command of ISAF in Kabul. It now aims to get the top-of-the-line NATO Reaction Force operational a year earlier than expected—and has no idea yet what the NRF might be asked to do or who should do the asking. Quarrels about the Iraq war that were almost fatal for NATO suggest that consensus among alliance members on going to war in ambiguous circumstances will be hard to attain. And it is inconceivable that non-U.S. contributors of young men and women to the NRF will cede exclusive control over its deployment to the world hegemon.

Is NATO doomed, then, to become nothing more than a superb tool-box for the United States (and sometimes the European interventionist nations of Britain and France) to choose from, if the chosen consent on a case-by-case basis? Will national units in the NRF excuse themselves from missions ad hoc?

More broadly, what should be the criteria for NATO out-of-Europe missions? So far NATO's global commitments have been made haphaz-ardly, with ill-defined obligations, and with no coherent rationale or set of priorities to determine when and where intervention is justified. Indeed, a major motivation in expanding alliance writ seems to have been less a reasoned calculation that the alliance is the best instrument for dealing with certain global tasks than a desperate attempt to save NATO in its hour of potential obsolescence by giving it new duties. This may be an honorable motive, but it provides no sure foundation for calibrating future activism.

To be sure, this lack of orientation is nothing new. In the post–cold war decade NATO evolved by doing first and philosophizing afterward. The standing joke about the Partnership for Peace, NATO's skin-of-its-teeth defeat of Slobodan Milosevic in Kosovo, and other innovations was, "This works in practice, but can it ever work in theory?" Yet in a world full of injustice, bloodshed, and failed states, NATO must devise some guide-lines for its triage. Should the West intervene militarily in Liberia, Sudan, or the Congo because failed states there could become the new havens for terrorists? In Peru? In Aceh?

And beyond military clarity—assuming that those Bush administra-tion hawks who do think that NATO is a touchstone have finally won over those hawks who say "good-riddance" and that the alliance's survival is thus assured—what should NATO's new political role be? Is it just to rub-ber-stamp decisions by the world's hyperpower? Should some system of majority voting be introduced to prevent maverick vetoes on premission decisions such as commissioning planners to design specific contingency scenarios? Or, as Americans and Europeans reevaluate the flaws of the

United Nations and the advantages of international legitimacy in sensitive situations, should NATO become a kind of western United Nations (as in Kosovo in 1999) to provide justification when "unreasonable" vetoes block Security Council sanction for "serious consequences"? Or would that only tar NATO as imperialist in the eyes of much of the Islamic "premodern" world?[36]

Europeans, looking at their own post-Iraq transformation, have almost as many questions about their tottering Common Foreign and Security Policy as they do about NATO. But one major conclusion has already emerged. It is that neither Blair's embrace of the hegemon nor Chirac's fulminations against it can serve Europe's purposes as long as Europe remains divided. The two leaders may well have had the same goal of braking Washington's more radical actions, but neither succeeded. French conceit that it is the natural leader of Europe is in any case not shared by other Europeans. And its compulsive defiance of the United States is seen as not only unrealistic, but also unserious and irritating.

As for Blair, he is increasingly seen by Europeans as the sacrificial lamb in the American obsession with controlling U.S. allies. He is perceived as having won nothing for his dogged loyalty except Washington's abortive turn to the United Nations in the fall of 2002 and (bilaterally) a promise of no death penalty for British citizens sentenced on terrorist charges in U.S. courts. When Blair was in severe political difficulty just before the Iraq war, Secretary of State Rumsfeld had no qualms about brushing off British forces as insignificant in the view of the powerful Americans. When Blair got into even greater postwar political trouble over prewar exaggeration of the dangers of Iraqi WMD—here European reportage on the issue differed sharply from American reportage—the Americans did not hesitate to make a scapegoat of British intelligence, in the European reading. And because of the political capital he had to spend on Iraq, Blair further lost the window of opportunity in which he might have been able to bring the British pound into the European Monetary Union as he wished to do.[37]

For many European policymakers, the logical deduction is that allegiance to Washington does not pay, and neither does defiance of Washington. In a unipolar world the only approach that might promote European interests and sensibilities would be a common European foreign policy that would have behind it all of Europe's economic weight, the equivalent of America's. The aim would be cooperation with the United States. The hope would be that the style of cooperation might revert from today's hierarchical hegemony to a more cold-war style participatory hegemony. This is quite different from the kind of anti-Gulliver emancipation from the hegemon that some prominent European intellectuals like Jürgen Habermas advocate—and that American observer Charles Kupchan expects Europe to be goaded into.[38] The mandarins, by and large, accept U.S. hegemony; they are glad to see the end of Saddam Hussein's nasty regime; rather than prolonging polemics about the past, they now want to work together in Iraq, but on a more international basis, and not as hirelings of the American military occupation.[39]

Just how long the present elite European consensus for cooperation might endure in the face of prolonged unrelenting American unilateralism, however, is not clear. The first signs of a more serious anti-Americanism among European professionals normally well disposed to the United States may perhaps be discerned in such declarations of independence as that by Heinrich Vogel, former director of the German Institute of Eastern Studies. America's determination "to preserve its own freedom from attack and freedom to attack" and its flaunting of "absolute military superiority," he writes, "has damaged the US claim to political leadership so profoundly that America's allies must now speak openly about their conditions for continued cooperation."[40] Armand Clesse, director of the Luxembourg Institute for European and International Studies, goes further in calling the United States an "autistic megalosaurus" bent on "world domination" (and calling the EU, for good measure, a "political eunuch").[41]

Within the EU, foreign policy, as distinct from economic policy, has always been the area that is least amenable to unity among such diverse EU members as Britain and France, with their histories of empires and expeditionary campaigns, and Sweden, with its centuries of peace. But in every area steps toward intensified integration have almost always been the result of crises, as atomized responses have proved futile, and the EC/EU has been forced to pool national sovereignties even more to amass the power to master the crises. European commissioner for enlargement Günter Verheugen speaks for many when he expects the same outcome this time from the "healthy shock" of the Europeans' disarray in foreign policy over the past two years.[42] It is probably safe to say that the mainstream west and central European diplomats anticipate that there will be no permanent split in foreign policy between "old" and "new" Europeans, but that the process of consensus building will winnow out agreed policies of working closely with the United States on such issues as revising the understanding of sovereign rights and preemptive defense under international law—while at the same time strengthening regimes like the International Criminal Court and the Kyoto Protocol that the Europeans adhere to but the Americans do not.[43]

Already the shock of their own and the transatlantic alliance's disarray has prodded EU members to write a common strategic assessment of threats—and a robust one at that—and to accept the need in some circumstances to use military force outside Europe in defense against the threats. Both steps would have been unthinkable before September 11, 2001. EU representatives, in talks with Iran, are now also putting more stress on the critical part of the dialogue, and they will withhold trade rewards unless Tehran accepts more intrusive inspections of its nuclear programs by the International Atomic Energy Agency.

On the other side of the Atlantic, the kind of transformation that may be working its way through the system is not yet obvious. On the eve of the Iraq war, favorable opinion about the United States plunged from 63 percent in mid-2002 to 31 percent in France, from 61 percent to 25 percent in Germany, and from 70 percent to 34 percent in Italy. Clearly this drop in U.S. popularity in the world, as an index of American loss of soft power, triggered no rethinking in Washington.[44] The U.S. administration still held that those who were not with the United States were against it and blamed the transatlantic breach of 2003 exclusively on French insolence and German ingratitude.

Yet the American rediscovery in postwar Iraq that you can do everything with bayonets except sit on them may now be different. To begin with, a cautious American-German reconciliation has begun, twelve months after the acrimonious German election. Foreign Minister Joschka Fischer, on his first post–Iraq war visit to Washington in July, got to see Vice President Cheney—an honor otherwise reserved in the previous year for Germany's opposition conservative politicians. And on this occasion the zeal of the Republican right for ostracizing Schröder palpably softened. Leaks began coming out of Washington that some of the new Europeans in central Europe were asking the United States not to push the Germans into national pacifism. President Bush himself, in remarks that made front-page news in Germany but were barely noticed in American media, lauded the Germans in early August for their service in commanding the ISAF forces in Afghanistan. And conservative American columnists began picking up the theme that Wolfgang Ischinger, German ambassador to the United States, preached throughout 2003—that in its own interest the United States should not shove Germany into France's arms and thus reinforce French defiance, but should entice Berlin to distance itself somewhat from Paris and return to its traditional position bridging American and French views. In exemplary fashion *Wall Street Journal* columnist George Melloan, for one, treated as a change of Berlin's policy Fischer's usual boilerplate message that Germany's "ideas about international politics . . . are precisely the opposite of Mr. Chirac's grand vision of a united Europe that would become a rival to the U.S. for global power." Fischer "said that Germany does not want to be a rival to the U.S. He asserted that Europe can only be strong in cooperation with the U.S., not as a competitor."[45]

The high point of bilateral rapprochement followed, as Bush received Schröder himself for forty minutes in a New York hotel in September. This hardly matched Vladimir Putin's two-day reception at Camp David later in the week. But it at least suggested a modulation in the White House maxim from ignoring the Germans to tolerating them—even though Schröder specified that no German troops would go to postwar Iraq and that Germany and Europe's financial contribution to reconstruction would be modest without some larger UN role there.

In substance, in his fall speech to the United Nations, Bush remained unwilling to dilute American control in Iraq, even for the reward of spreading the risk, and chose instead to forgo troop contributions to peacekeeping in Iraq from countries that insisted on a larger UN role.[46] Europeans who had opposed the war held back correspondingly, and with no French or German forces going to Iraq, and no significantly greater political scope for the United Nations there, countries such as Pakistan, India, and South Korea, whom the United States had hoped would send forces, exhibited equal reluctance.

Far more of a setback for the Bush administration was the change of climate in America. The sharp drop in trust in the U.S. around the world—by fall huge majorities in Britain and every other European country except Poland disapproved of U.S. foreign policy, while only 7 percent of Saudis and only 15 percent of Indonesians, down from 61 percent a year earlier, approved of U.S. policy—was bearable for a superpower.[47] What was not bearable were the new opinion surveys in the United States itself showing that almost as many voters now disapproved of the Iraq war in retrospect as approved of it; up to two-thirds thought the American military presence in the Middle East increased rather than decreased the likelihood of terrorism; and 81 percent thought the United States should work more closely with other countries to combat terrorism. Increasing numbers resented the mobilization of still more National Guard units for duty in Iraq and the additional $1,000-a-year bill their families would have to pay if other lands did not share costs with the United States in Iraq.[48] They feared a new quagmire and were suspicious of the president's request for supplemental $87 billion appropriations (primarily for operations in Iraq and Afghanistan) that would push public debt up to $525 billion and the fiscal deficit up to 6 percent of GDP. Bush's personal disapproval rating shot up almost as high as his sagging approval ratings, with the CNN-USA Today-Gallup poll showing 47 percent and 50 percent respectively.[49]

As Bush's popularity slipped, various Democrats and even centrist Republicans became emboldened. After a four-month investigation, both parties' leaders of the House of Representative's intelligence committee concluded jointly that the intelligence on which the United States went to war in Iraq was outdated.[50] Joseph Biden, ranking Democrat on the Senate foreign relations committee, Clinton's secretary of state, Madeleine Albright, and Jimmy Carter's national security adviser, Zbigniew Brzezinski, all gave the first coherent outlines of what could become an alternative Democratic foreign policy.[51] What Yale's Paul Kennedy labeled a "supine Congress" seemed to be sitting up.[52]

More surprisingly, cracks began to appear among the neoconservatives; in particular, *Weekly Standard* editor William Kristol began savaging Defense Secretary Donald Rumsfeld.[53] Bush was losing his Teflon shield, it seemed, and the neoconservatives were losing their hitherto imposing control of the agenda. A summons to patriotism no longer rallied politicians and the public behind administration policies on the familiar pattern of the previous two years.

The event that revealed the slippage most dramatically was the resurfacing of the Wilson affair in ways that uncannily paralleled the David Kelly affair in Britain. In September it suddenly became known that the CIA had asked the Justice Department to investigate the exposure of Valerie Plame as a CIA operative the previous July—a crime rating a ten-year jail sentence under American law. Plame's husband, Joseph C. Wilson, the whistleblower on the forgeries behind the "yellowcake" charge repeated in Bush's 2003 State of the Union address, publicly suspected no less than Bush's campaign manager, Karl Rove, of having masterminded the leak.[54] Both the Democrats and the Washington press corps, as the BBC put it, scented blood. Personification of disputes was much more fun than abstract policy debates and allowed for more facile win-lose tallies.

At this point Europeans by no means expected the United States to rediscover the charms of permanent coalitions of steady allies over coalitions of the temporarily willing. They did entertain the hope, however, that a somewhat less monolithic Washington might now be emerging that would provide openings for them to rejoin American foreign-policy deliberations.

After the wars of 2003 there can be no easy return to the voluntary transatlantic alliance system Washington built up over half a century to maximize U.S. influence abroad by the soft power of persuading others to want what the United States wants. Nor can there be a return to what then looked like existential danger but now seems like the much simpler peace of the cold war. But one can at least hope that there is enough trust left, or that enough trust can be rebuilt, between the natural allies of the United States and Europe to prevent the next clash too from being fatal.

We could do worse than remember Dean Acheson's quiet postscript to a tribute Winston Churchill once paid America. Acheson related that he heard "Churchill say 'that the hope of the world lies in the strength and will of the United States.' He would not object to my adding—and in its good judgment as well."[55]

NOTES

Preface

1. Henry A. Kissinger, "Role Reversal and Alliance Realities," *Washington Post,* March 27, 2003, pp. 6–10. All *Washington Post* articles are from the *Washington Post* website, www.washingtonpost.com.

2. Timothy Garton Ash, "Anti-Europeanism in America," *New York Review of Books,* March 27, 2003, pp. 6–10.

3. This view was expressed by, among others, *Weekly Standard* editor William Kristol in various Washington seminars in April 2002.

4. Conversation with the editor, May 2002.

5. See, for example, Karsten D. Voigt, "US-EU: Putting Transatlantic Relations to the Test?" *Transatlantic Internationale Politik* (German Council on Foreign Relations), vol. 3, no. 3 (Fall 2002), pp. 35–39.

6. Testimony to the European Subcommittee of the House Committee on International Relations, June 11, 2003, wwwa.house.gov/international_relations/108/ham0611.htm.

7. For a sampling of the numerous exasperated media commentaries about the juvenile behavior of today's leaders, see the *New York Times* editorial, "Shadow over the Summit," June 1, 2003; Michael O'Hanlon, "Why Rumsfeld Should Lay Off the French," *International Herald Tribune,* May 30, 2003, p. 6; and Maureen Dowd, "No More Bratwurst!" *New York Times,* September 25, 2002. All *New York Times* articles are from the *New York Times* website, www.nytimes.com.

8. Joseph P. Quinlan, *Drifting Apart or Growing Together? The Primacy of the Transatlantic Economy* (Washington: Center for Transatlantic Relations, 2003).

Chapter One

1. Robert Kagan, "Power and Weakness," *Policy Review,* no. 113, June and July 2002, revised as the book *Of Paradise and Power* (Knopf, 2003); "Wachsende Kluft innerhalb der NATO" (Growing chasm inside NATO) and "Marke mit

Imageproblem" (A brand with an image problem), *Süddeutsche Zeitung*, February 4, 2002, pp. 1, 2; "Abermals Warnungen in Richtung Bagdad" (Yet again warnings to Baghdad), *Frankfurter Allgemeine Zeitung*, February 4, 2002, p. 1; Steven Erlanger, "U.S. Officials Try to Assure Europeans on NATO," *New York Times*, February 3, 2002.

2. See, for example, *Survival*, vol. 43, no. 4 (Winter 2001–02).

3. For one examination of the U.S.-NATO strains after American rejection of the offer, see Anne Deighton, "The Eleventh of September and Beyond: NATO," in Lawrence Freedman, ed., *Superterrorism: Policy Responses* (Oxford: Blackwell, 2002).

4. www.whitehouse.gov/news/releases/2002/01/20020129-11.html.

5. That controversy would hit the streets only a month later. Eric Schmitt, "U.S. Tries to Dampen Fear Abroad on Policy," *New York Times*, March 11, 2002.

6. John B. Judis and Spencer Ackerman, "The Selling of the Iraq War," *New Republic* online, post date June 19, 2003, issue date June 30, 2003, www.tnr.com/docprint.mhtml?i=20030630&s=ackermanjudis063003.

7. "Powell's Moment," *Washington Post*, February 10, 2002.

8. Robert Cooper, "How Shall We Answer Robert Kagan?" *Transatlantic Internationale Politik*, vol. 4, no. 2 (Summer 2003), pp. 19–24.

9. Paul Kennedy, *The Rise and Fall of the Great Powers* (Random House, 1987).

10. Joseph S. Nye Jr., *Bound to Lead* (Basic Books, 1990).

11. Published in book form as *The End of History and the Last Man* (Free Press, 1992).

12. Kagan, "Power and Weakness."

13. See International Institute for Strategic Studies, *Strategic Survey 2002/3* (London: 2003), p. 69.

14. So much so that Adam Garfinkle, then editor of the neoconservatives' highbrow foreign-policy journal *The National Interest*, rejected Kagan's article as too obvious before Kagan found another outlet. Author's conversation with Garfinkle, September 2002.

15. This was articulated most coherently by Michael Doyle in his *Ways of War and Peace* (W. W. Norton, 1997).

16. Karl Kaiser, "The New World Order," *Transatlantic Internationale Politik*, vol. 4, no. 2 (Summer 2003), pp. 3–9.

17. Joseph S. Nye Jr., *The Paradox of American Power* (Oxford University Press, 2002).

18. "Mars and Venus Reconciled: A New Era for Transatlantic Relations," lecture at Harvard's Kennedy School of Government, April 7, 2003, http://ue.eu.int/solana/list.asp?BID=107.

19. Testimony to the European Subcommittee of the House Committee on International Relations, June 11, 2003, wwwa.house.gov/international_relations/108/Serf0611.pdf.

20. Philip Gordon, "Bridging the Atlantic Divide," *Foreign Affairs*, vol. 82, no. 1 (January/February 2003), pp. 70–83.

21. Robert Cooper, *The Post-Modern State and the World Order* (London: Demos, 1996).

22. J. H. H. Weiler, "The Transformation of Europe," *Yale Law Journal*, vol. 100, no. 2 (1991), p. 403.

23. J. H. H. Weiler, *The Constitution of Europe* (Cambridge University Press, 1999); Albert O. Hirschman, *Exit, Voice, and Loyalty* (Harvard University Press, 1970).

24. For a good description of this particular battlefield from the neoconservative point of view, see Gerard Baker, "The Neo-Cons Did Not Hijack US Policy," *Financial Times*, June 19, 2003, p. 15. *Financial Times* articles are from the European print edition.

25. This assessment of the evolution in European thinking is based on interviews conducted from September 2001 through June 2003.

26. Cited in Marina Ottoway, "Think Again: Nation-Building," *Foreign Policy* (September/October 2002), www.globalpolicy.org/nations/future-2002/0910building.htm.

27. "2d Presidential Debate between Gov. Bush and Vice President Gore," *New York Times*, October 12, 2000.

28. Bob Woodward, *Bush at War* (Simon & Schuster, 2002), pp. 84–85.

29. Popular worry about terrorist attacks rose to similar 40 percentiles in France, Germany, Great Britain, and the United States, with the German 46 percent surpassing even the American 45 percent. When other pollsters phrased questions differently, the number of Europeans expecting terrorist attacks even rose to two-thirds. Pew Research Center, Eurobarometer, and Gallup surveys after 9/11, as collated and analyzed by Frauke N. Bielka and Christian Tuschoff, "Common Threats—Diverging Responses," American Institute for Contemporary German Studies, Washington, April 2002.

30. TREVI is the French acronym for terrorism, radicalism, extremism, and internal violence. See John D. Occhipinti, "The Impact of Enlargement on Justice and Home Affairs," paper presented at the EUSA conference in Nashville, March 29, 2003, and *The Politics of EU Police Cooperation* (Boulder, Colo.: Lynne Rienner, 2003).

31. For an analysis of Blair and the British elite's position as a "hinge" between the United States and Europe, see Anatol Lieven, *The Hinge to Europe: Don't Make Britain Choose between the U.S. and the E.U.*, Policy Brief 25 (Carnegie Endowment, August, 2003).

32. Pew and Eurobarometer reports, in Bielka and Tuschoff, "Common Threats."

33. *Le Monde*, September 13, 2001, p. 1.

34. "Ground Zero," *Transatlantic Internationale Politik*, vol. 2, no. 4 (Winter 2001), p. 1.

35. www.worldviews.org.

36. Seymour Martin Lipset, *American Exceptionalism* (W. W. Norton, 1996); Walter Russell Mead, *Special Providence: American Foreign Policy and How It*

Changed the World (New York: Century Foundation Book, 2002); Francis Fukuyama, "Has History Restarted since September 11?" John Bonython Lecture at the Centre for Independent Studies, Melbourne, Australia, August 8, 2002.

37. See, for example, Daniel Gros, "Europe's Problem Is Not the Stability Pact," *Financial Times*, October 24, 2002, p. 15. *Financial Times* articles are from the European print edition. For a dissenting New Labour view that a two-decade comparison and more analogous data suggest much more U.S.-European equivalence in productivity than do the 1990s alone, see Will Hutton, *The World We're In* (London: Little, Brown, 2002).

38. Pierre Hassner, "Friendly Questions to America the Powerful," *In the National Interest*, vol. 1, no. 2 (Fall 2002), www.inthenationalinterest.com; and *The United States: The Empire of Force or the Force of Empire?* Chaillot paper 54 (Paris: EU Institute for Security Studies, September 2002), www.iss-eu.org.

39. The Chicago Council on Foreign Relations/German Marshall Fund of the US survey found that in May 2002, 91 percent of Americans saw international terrorism as a threat, while "only" 64 percent of Europeans did; 86 percent of Americans saw Iraqi development of WMD as a threat, as against "only" 57 percent of Europeans. *Worldviews 2002*, publication date not given.

40. Michael Howard, *The Invention of Peace* (Yale University Press, 2000); John Mueller, *Retreat from Doomsday: The Obsolescence of Major War* (Basic Books, 1989); Paul Johnson, "World War II and the Path to Peace," *Wall Street Journal Europe*, May 8, 1995, p. 6; Pierre Hassner, "Beyond the Three Traditions: The Philosophy of War and Peace in Historical Perspective," *International Affairs*, vol. 70, no. 4 (October 1994), pp. 737–56. Michael Mandelbaum also addressed the issue in *The Dawn of Peace in Europe* (New York: Twentieth Century Fund, 1996) and *The Ideas That Conquered the World: Peace, Democracy, and Free Markets in the Twenty-First Century* (New York: Public Affairs, 2002), but paid minimal attention to the EC/EU, which has carried these ideas further than any other part of the world.

41. See, for example, Anne Applebaum, "Listen to Germany," *Washington Post*, February 5, 2003, p. A23. Even literature was not exempt from this reflex. When Günter Grass published his fictional rendering of the Soviet torpedo sinking in 1945 of the *Wilhelm Gustloff*, with the loss of more than 8,000 German refugees aboard, many English-language reviews and news articles seemed to think this was the first time that German authors had dared to write about the brutal expulsions and deaths of hundreds of thousands of German civilians from the Sudetenland and old Prussia after Hitler's defeat—and speculated that the novel signaled a new German self-confidence and assertiveness. The book appeared in English as *Crabwalk* (Harcourt, 2003).

42. Fritz René Allemann, *Bonn Ist Nicht Weimar* (Bonn is not Weimar) (Cologne: Kiepenheuer & Witsch, 1956; reissued in 2000 in Frankfurt by R. G. Fischer).

43. Heinrich August Winkler, *Der lange Weg nach Westen* (The long road to the West) (Munich: Beck, 2000).

44. Karl Dietrich Bracher and others, eds., *Geschichte der Bundesrepublik Deutschland* (History of the Federal Republic of Germany) (Stuttgart/Mannheim: Deutsche Verlags-Anstalt/F. A. Brockhaus, last volume released in 1987).

45. Timothy Garton Ash, *In Europe's Name* (Random House, 1993).

46. For my own generally positive assessment, see Elizabeth Pond, *The Rebirth of Europe*, rev. ed. (Brookings, 2002).

47. Paul Krugman, "Stating the Obvious," *New York Times*, May 27, 2003; Grover G. Norquist, "Step-by-Step Tax Reform," *Washington Post*, June 9, 2003; David S. Broder, "Tipping the Republicans' Hand?" *Washington Post*, June 18, 2003, p. A25.

48. Charles Krauthammer, "The Unipolar Moment," *Foreign Affairs*, vol. 70, no. 1 (winter 1990–91), pp. 23–33.

49. Patrick E. Tyler, "U.S. Strategic Plan Calls for Ensuring No Rivals Develop," *New York Times*, March 8, 1992.

50. William Kristol and Robert Kagan, "Toward a Neo-Reaganite Foreign Policy," *Foreign Affairs*, vol. 75, no. 4 (July/August 1996), pp. 18–32.

51. Joseph Cirincione, "Origins of Regime Change in Iraq," Carnegie Proliferation Brief, vol. 6, no. 5 (March 19, 2003), www.ceip.org/files/Publications/Originsofregimechangeiniraq.asp?from=pubtype; Bill Keller, "Is It Good for the Jews?" March 8, 2003, www.nytimes.com/ 2003/03/08/opinion/08KELL.html; Walter Laqueur, "Amerikas Neokonservative sind keine bösen Geister" (America's neoconservatives are no evil spirits), *Die Welt*, June 12, 2003, p. 6. ; and Elizabeth Drew, "The Neoconservatives in Power," *New York Review of Books*, vol. 50, no. 10 (June 12, 2003). For a German take on the neoconservative phenomenon, see Stefan Fröhlich, "Hegemonialer Internationalismus" (Hegemonial internationalsim), *Frankfurter Allgemeine Zeitung*, April 10, 2003, p. 8.

52. Washington, September, 2000, available at www.newamericancentury.org. For an argument that the real driving force behind the neoconservative push to war in Iraq was in fact concern about the stability of the world's top Saudi producer of oil—and a desire to shift America's prime military and oil-supply base in the Mideast to the world's number-two producer, Iraq—see Jeffrey Sachs, "The Real Target of the War in Iraq Was Saudi Arabia," *Financial Times*, August 13, 2002, p. 11.

53. Steven Mufson and Thomas E. Ricks, "Debate over Targets Highlights Difficulties," *Washington Post*, September 21, 2001, p. A25.

Chapter Two

1. Chris Patten, "Jaw-Jaw, not War-War," *Financial Times*, February 14, 2002.

2. Will Hutton, "Time to Stop Being America's Lap-Dog," *Observer*, February 17, 2002. All *Observer* and *Guardian* articles in this book were accessed at www.observer.co.uk.

3. Charles Grant, "Powerless Europe," *Prospect* (March 2002), pp. 12–13.

4. The best-known prediction of a nuclear Germany was John Mearsheimer's

"Back to the Future: Instability in Europe after the Cold War," *International Security*, vol. 15, no. 1 (Summer 1990), pp. 5–56.

5. Joseph S. Nye Jr., *The Paradox of American Power* (Oxford University Press, 2002), p. 36.

6. See exchanges about "balancing" and "bandwagoning" in *International Security*, especially Josef Joffe, "'Bismarck' or Britain? Toward an American Grand Strategy after Bipolarity," *International Security*, vol. 19, no. 4 (Spring 1995), pp. 94–117; and Josef Joffe, "Power Lies in the Balancing," *Australian*, August 6, 2003, carried in NATO Enlargement Daily Brief, August 7, 2003, archived in http://groups.yahoo.com/group/nedb/messages.

7. Author's interview, June 2003. For an exposition of Schäuble's concerns about the transatlantic alliance, see his Scheitert der Westen? (Will the West fail?) (Gütersloh: Bertelsmann, 2003).

8. *After Victory* (Princeton University Press, 2001), pp. 257–59. See also his article, "America's Imperial Ambition," in *Foreign Affairs*, vol. 81, no. 5 (September/ October 2002), pp. 44–60.

9. Dean Acheson, *Present at the Creation* (W. W. Norton, 1969), pp. 725, 728, 737.

10. Insiders distinguish between the two Bush presidents by their number as president of the United States. George H. W. Bush was the forty-first president, George W. the forty-third.

11. For accounts of how this soft landing was achieved, see Philip Zelikow and Condoleezza Rice, *Germany Unified and Europe Transformed* (Harvard University Press, 1997); and Elizabeth Pond, *Beyond the Wall* (Brookings, 1993). In today's context, a major difference between the two books is that Zelikow and Rice attribute the soft landing to U.S. government resolve that brooked no opposition as Washington steered unfolding events, while Pond attributes the soft landing to the extraordinarily close and sensitive cooperation between the American and German governments in working out modalities to give the central European populations what they already yearned for.

12. See Weiler's fascinating aside about the relation of law and maturity, being and becoming, obedience and freedom, "doing" and "hearkening," as the Hebrews wandered in the wilderness for forty years after their exodus from Egypt. J. H. H. Weiler, *The Constitution of Europe: "Do the New Clothes Have an Emperor?" and Other Essays on European Integration* (Cambridge University Press, 1999), pp. 6–9.

13. Conversation with author, March 2003.

14. The slur "wets" was popularized by Prime Minister Margaret Thatcher as a negative epithet for members of the Tory Party whom she deemed too far to the left.

15. Richard Perle, "What Do EU Know about the Fight on Terror, Mr Patten?" London *Sun*, February 16, 2002.

16. The point that they do not constitute a "school" seems to be an important one for neoconservatives. Irving Kristol, in "The Neoconservative Persuasion," *Weekly Standard*, August 25, 2003, argues that there is no neoconservative "move-

ment," but rather a neoconservative "persuasion" (www.aei.org/news/ newsID.19032/news_detail.asp).

17. Conference on The State of the Euro-Atlantic Partnership held at the American Enterprise Institute, Washington, December 4, 2002, text distributed on www.aei.org/nai.

18. Interview with Josef Joffe, "Der Sturz Saddams könnte heilsam sein" (The overthrow of Saddam could be healthy), *Die Zeit*, December 12, 2002, p. 4.

19. Aspen Institute talk, Berlin, September 16, 2002. For a sample of European coverage of official denials that the United States was acting unilaterally in early 2002, see also "Irritationen zwischen Paris und Washington/Amerikanische Demarchen gegen die Unilateralismus-Kritik" (Irritation between Paris and Washington/American demarches against criticism of unilateralism), *Neue Zürcher Zeitung*, February 19, 2002.

20. Richard Haass, cited in Judy Dempsey and Richard Wolffe, "Differences of Style," *Financial Times*, July 27, 2001, p. 16.

21. *Economist*, cited by Joseph Nye, *In the National Interest* online, June 2002.

22. Stanley Sloan, *In the National Interest* online, March 2003.

23. Ivo Daalder, reviewing Robert Kagan, "Americans Are from Mars, Europeans from Venus," *New York Times*, March 5, 2003.

24. Michael Lind, "Liberal Disunity Will Keep US Conservatives on Top," *Financial Times*, December 27, 2002, p. 9.

25. Charles Krauthammer, "The Unipolar Moment Revisited," *The National Interest*, no. 70 (Winter 2002/03); and Joseph S. Nye Jr., "A Whole New Ball Game," *Financial Times*, December 28, 2002, p. 1.

26. Niall Ferguson took a revisionist look at the benefits of the British Empire in *Empire: How Britain Made the Modern World* (London: Allen Lane, 2003). Novelist, human-rights professor, and disciple of Isaiah Berlin, Michael Ignatieff wrote *Empire Lite: Nation Building in Bosnia, Kosovo, Afghanistan* (Vintage, 2003). Andrew Bacevich argued that America has actually been assembling an empire, not accidentally, but deliberately, for a century, in *American Empire: The Realities and Consequences of US Diplomacy* (Harvard University Press, 2002). Robert Jervis surmised that this is what powerful nations invariably do, in "The Compulsive Empire," *Foreign Policy*, no. 137 (July/August, 2003), pp. 82–87.

27. Quoted by Paul Kennedy, "Has the US Lost Its Way?" *Observer*, March 3, 2002.

28. Philip Stephens, "The World Needs a Confident America, not a Fearful One," *Financial Times*, December 13, 2002, p. 19; and Philip Stephens, "Present at the Destruction of the World's Partnership," *Financial Times*, March 7, 2003, p. 15. Even after the occupation of Iraq turned sour in the summer of 2003, Blair continued to maintain that the United States had acted multilaterally in going to war, because Britain and all the small partners, who together put up 1 percent of the troops, joined Washington in the campaign.

29. For a good EU think-tank overview of U.S.-European relations in mid-2002, see Julian Lindley-French, "Terms of Engagement" (Paris: EU Institute for Security Studies, Chaillot Paper 52, May 2002).

30. Author's conversation with Guillaume Parmentier, director of the French Center on the United States at the French Institute for International Relations, June 2003.

31. "Die Struck-Doktrin" (The Struck doctrine), *Frankfurter Allgemeine Zeitung*, December 6, 2002, p. 1.

32. Cited in Kori Schake and Klaus Becher, "How America Should Lead," *Policy Review*, no. 114 (August/September), 2002, www.policyreview.org/AUG02/schake_print.html.

33. Chris Patten, "America Should Not Relinquish Respect," *Financial Times*, October 3, 2002, p. 15.

34. Zbigniew Brzezinski, "Where Do We Go from Here?" *Transatlantic Internationale Politik*, vol. 4, no. 3 (Fall 2003), pp. 3–10.

35. Chris Stephen, "Operation Anaconda," *Prospect*, December 2002, pp. 52–54. For an evaluation of the Afghan campaign that sees Operation Anaconda as only a blip in a brilliant overall campaign, see Michael E. O'Hanlon, "A Flawed Masterpiece," *Foreign Affairs*, vol. 81, no. 3 (May/June 2002), pp. 47–63. For CIA-Pentagon rivalry in the military campaign, see David Ignatius, "A Covert Turf War," *Washington Post*, January 21, 2003, p. 11.

36. For a more positive evaluation of nation building in Afghanistan in mid-2003, see Edward Luce and Victoria Burnett, "Afghanistan's Slow Progress: 'Contrary to the General Expectation, We Have Been Able to Make Things Happen,'" *Financial Times*, July 17, 2003, p. 11.

37. For one withering British comment, see Peter Beaumont, "American cant," *Observer*, January 13, 2002, www.observer.co.uk/comment/story/0,6903, 631883,00.html. See also Constanze Stelzenmüller, "Justizfarce im Niemandsland" (Farcical justice in no-man's land), *Die Zeit*, July 31, 2003, p. 5.

38. After the American-French clash in the run-up to the Iraq war in 2003, National Security Adviser Rice put it most bluntly in an interview with *Le Monde*: "There were times that it appeared that American power was seen to be more dangerous than, perhaps, Saddam Hussein. . . . We simply didn't understand it." "Rice Repeats U.S. Complaints about France," Reuters, May 31, 2003, carried in NATO Enlargement Daily Brief, May 31, 2003, put out by the Latvian Embassy in Washington, archived at http://groups.yahoo.com/group/nedb/messages.

39. Jeffrey Gedmin, "The Alliance Is Doomed," *Washington Post*, May 19, 2002.

40. Charles Krauthammer, "Re-Imagining NATO," *Washington Post*, May 24, 2002, p. A35.

41. Newt Gingrich, "Rogue State Department," *Foreign Policy*, no. 137 (July/August 2003), pp. 42–49.

42. At the American Enterprise Institute symposium on "The End of the West?" November 28, 2002, transcript distributed by www.aei.org/nai.

43. Henry A. Kissinger, "The 'Made in Berlin' Generation," *Washington Post*, October 30, 2002, p. A23, as quoted in Stephen Szabo, "A Poisoned Victory? German-American Relations and the Election of 2002," in David P. Conradt and

others, eds., *A Precarious Victory: Schroeder and the German Elections of 2002* (manuscript).

44. *Guardian*, January 22, 2003. "Your eyes have gone out and your nose/ Sniffs only the pong of the dead/And all the dead air is alive/With the smell of America's God."

45. John Lloyd, "How Anti-Americanism Betrays the Left," *Observer*, March 17, 2003.

46. Jochen Bittner, "Blackbox Weisses Haus," (Blackbox White House), *Die Zeit*, July 24, 2003, p. 5.

47. "Dunkle Mächte" (Dark powers), *Der Spiegel*, August 4, 2003, www.Spiegel.de/Spiegel/0,1518,259727,00.html.

48. Dan Diner, *Feindbild Amerika* (Munich: Propyläen, 2002).

49. "European-US Relations under the Spotlight," World Economic Forum press release from Davos, January 25, 2003.

50. Testimony before the Congressional Subcommittee on Europe of the House Committee on International Relations, June 17, 2003, available at www.brookings.edu.

51. Michael Mertes, "German Anti-Americanism? Forget It!" *Transatlantic Internationale Politik*, vol. 4, no. 4 (Winter 2003).

52. *Worldviews 2002*, cosponsored by the Chicago Council on Foreign Relations and the German Marshall Fund of the United States, Chicago, Washington, 2002. For contrary views, see, for example, Michael Gonzalez, "How We Got Here," *Wall Street Journal Europe*, April 9, 2003, looking at France and Belgium; and Klaus-Dieter Frankenberger, "Partnerschaft in der Krise/Der Antiamerikanismus ist in Europa so populär wie seit Jahrzehnten nicht mehr" (Partnership in crisis/Anti-Americanism is more popular in Europe than it has been for decades), *Frankfurter Allgemeine Zeitung*, September 11, 2002, p. 3, looking at Germany.

53. As of June 30, 2003, the death toll was 806 Israelis and 2,414 Palestinians since the outbreak of the second *intifada* in 2000. Roughly similar proportions had prevailed throughout the *intifada*. AP, "Chain of Events in the Middle East Conflict," *Washington Post*, June 30, 2003.

54. Charles Krauthammer, "Europe and 'Those People,'" *Washington Post*, April 26, 2002, p. A29. See also Christopher Caldwell, "Liberté, Egalité, Judaeophobie," *Weekly Standard*, cited in Tony Judt, "The Way We Live Now," *New York Review of Books*, March 27, 2003, pp. 6–10.

55. Thomas L. Friedman, "Nine Wars Too Many," *New York Times*, May 15, 2002. See also George F. Will, "'Final Solution,' Phase 2," *Washington Post*, May 2, 2002, p. A23; William Safire, "The German Problem," *New York Times*, September 19, 2002; and Caldwell, "Liberté, Egalité, Judaeophobie."

56. Jonah Goldberg, *National Review Online*, July 16, 2002, cited in Timothy Garton Ash, "Anti-Europeanism in America," *New York Review of Books*, March 27, 2003, pp. 6–10.

57. "Amerika, du machst es besser/Warum Juden in aller Welt lieber auf die US-

Armee vertrauen als auf Friedensbewegungen" (America, you do it better/Why Jews in the whole world would rather trust the US Army than peace movements), *Die Zeit,* January 23, 2003, p. 29.

58. Linda Grant, "America's Liberal Jews," *Prospect,* no. 84 (March 2003), pp. 53–54.

59. Antony Lerman, "Sense on Antisemitism," *Prospect,* no. 77, August 2002, pp. 34–39. For other voices in this debate, see Anatol Lieven, "Speaking Up," *Prospect,* vol. 86 (May 2003), pp. 24–27; Michael Lind, "The Israel Lobby," *Prospect,* vol. 73 (April 2002), pp. 22–29; and Michael Brenner, "Juden und Normalität" (Jews and normality), *Süddeutsche Zeitung,* August 14, 2003, p, 13.

60. Tony Judt, "The Way We Live Now," *New York Review of Books,* March 27, 2003, pp. 6–10. Judt cites ADL websites and the 2002 Chicago Council on Foreign Relations survey.

61. John Lloyd, "Sign of Life from the Past?" *Financial Times,* November 16, 2002, p. I. See also Ian Buruma, "How To Talk about Israel," *New York Times Magazine,* August 31, 2003; and Dana H. Allin and Steven Simon, "The Moral Psychology of US Support for Israel," *Survival,* vol. 45, no. 3 (Autumn 2003), pp. 123–44.

62. John Lloyd, "Rowing Alone," *Financial Times,* August 3, 2002, p. I.

63. Richard Lambert, "Misunderstanding Each Other," *Foreign Affairs,* vol. 82, no. 2 (March-April 2003), pp. 62–74.

64. Michael Ledeen, "A Theory /What if There's Method to the Franco-German Madness?" *National Review,* March 11, 2003. Retired American colonel Ralph Peters matched Ledeen's wrath in comparing today's Germans with Joseph Goebbels; damning Europe's influence as "nothing but a heritage of nightmares"; proclaiming, "We will no longer stand for your blood-stained, rotten rules for the international system, but write our own rules"; and concluding sarcastically: "You have declared your independence from America. Now you have it. Lots of luck!" Ralph Peters, "Hitler War Wenigstens Ehrlich" (Hitler was at least honest), *Frankfurter Allgemeine Zeitung,* May 15, 2003, p. 31.

65. Garton Ash, "Anti-Europeanism in America."

66. See www.whitehouse.gov/news/releases/2002/06/20020601-3.html.

Chapter Three

1. For a skeptical German view of the possibilities of Iraqi democracy, see Udo Steinbach, "The Iraqi Fata Morgana," *Transatlantic Internationale Politik,* vol. 4, no. 3 (Fall 2003), pp. 73–78.

2. Samuel Huntington, *The Clash of Civilizations and the Remaking of World Order* (Touchstone, 1998).

3. Comments of Gen. Anthony Zinni (ret.) during a speech before the Florida Economic Club, August 23, 2002, www.npr.org/programs/morning/zinni.html; James A. Baker III, "The Right Way to Change a Regime," *New York Times,* August 25, 2002; Brent Scowcroft, "Don't Attack Saddam," *Wall Street Journal,* August 15, 2002; Nicholas Lemann, "The War on What?" *New Yorker,* Sept 16, 2002.

4. Online *Daily Standard* of August 26, 2002. The speech, entitled "Vice President Speaks at VFW 103rd National Convention," is available at www.whitehouse. gov/news/releases/2002/08/20020826.html.

5. On the lack of any significant American opposition to war in Iraq and the administration's masterful control of the political agenda, see, for example, Robert G. Kaiser, "There's a Reason Why There Hasn't Been Much of a Fight," *Washington Post*, February 16, 2003, p. B1. For an exploration of the absence of the kind of opposition that might have come from liberal Jewish organizations a decade earlier, see Anatol Lieven, "Speaking Up," *Prospect*, vol. 86 (May 2003), pp. 24–27.

6. Steven Erlanger, "Traces of Terror," *New York Times*, September 1, 2002. Indicating that the issue of war in Iraq was still wide open, this article noted: "Senior officials in Washington are angry at his [Schröder's] presumption that the American debate over Iraq is finished and his failure to give his closest ally the benefit of the doubt."

7. Author's background conversations with German officials.

8. Michael R. Gordon, "U.S. Air Raids in '02 Prepared for War in Iraq," *New York Times*, July 20, 2003.

9. Bob Woodward, *Bush at War* (Simon & Schuster, 2002), p. 38.

10. David Frum, *The Right Man* (Random House, 2003), p. 62.

11. Jim Hoagland, "How He Got Here," *Washington Post*, March 21, 2003, p. A37.

12. Zbigniew Brzezinski, "Where Do We Go from Here?" *Transatlantic Internationale Politik*, vol. 4, no. 3 (Fall 2003), pp. 3–10.

13. Thomas L. Friedman, "Chicken à la Iraq," *New York Times*, March 5, 2003.

14. Nicholas Lemann, "How It Came to War," *New Yorker*, March 31, 2003, pp. 36–40. See also James Harding, "The Figure in the White House Shadows Who Urged the President to War in Iraq," *Financial Times*, March 22, 2003, p. 9.

15. "Cheney bezeichnet den Irak als 'tödliche Gefahr,'" *Frankfurter Allgemeine Zeitung*, August 28, p. 1.

16. "Auch die Union ist gegen einen amerikanischen Alleingang," *Frankfurter Allgemeine Zeitung*, August 29, p. 1.

17. "Bundesregierung rückt von Hilfszusagen an Amerika ab," *Frankfurter Allgemeine Zeitung*, August 30, p. 1.

18. "Im Falle eines amerikanischen Angriffs will Berlin die Spürpanzer abziehen," and "Im deutschen Interesse," *Frankfurter Allgemeine Zeitung*, August 31, p. 1.

19. "Europäer: Vorrang für Diplomatie/ Unterschiedliche Optionen," and "Lob aus Bagdad," September 3, p. 1; and "Rollenspiel oder Konflikt?/Differenzen der amerikanischen Regierung in der Irak-Politik," *Frankfurter Allgemeine Zeitung*, September 3, p. 3.

20. "Schröder bekräftigt seine Irak-Politik/Amerika zweifelt an Enge der Beziehungen," *Frankfurter Allgemeine Zeitung*, September 5, p. 1.

21. Schröder bekräftigt uneingeschränkte Solidarität," *Frankfurter Allgemeine Zeitung*, September 7, 2002, p. 1; "Bushs Mann in Berlin ist nicht zum Leisetreten

da," and "Glaubenskrieg," *Frankfurter Allgemeine Zeitung*, September 7, 2002, p. 3.

22. The formulator of the phrase "civilian power" was Hanns W. Maull, in "Germany and Japan: The New Civilian Powers," *Foreign Affairs*, vol. 69, no. 5 (Winter 1990/91), pp. 91–106.

23. Author's background interviews. Javier Solana also expressed some concern about the transatlantic gap in this area in an interview with the *Financial Times*, "Solana Laments Rift between Europe and 'Religious' US," January 8, 2003, p. 14. See also Frank Bruni, "For President, a Mission and a Role in History," *New York Times*, September 22, 2001.

24. Victoria Clarke, "The Christian Zionists," *Prospect*, vol. 88 (July 2003), pp. 54–58; "US Policy and the Israeli-Palestinian Dispute/Re-engagement after Iraq?" IISS *Strategic Comments*, vol. 9, no. 2 (March 2003); and the Christian Zionist homepage, http://christianactionforisrael.org/index.html. The most prominent politician among Christian Zionists is House Majority Leader Tom DeLay. See David Firestone, "DeLay Is to Carry Dissenting Message on a Mideast Tour," *New York Times*, July 25, 2003; and James Bennet, "Palestinians Must Bear Burden of Peace, DeLay Tells Israelis," *New York Times*, July 31, 2003. For a popularization of the eschatology of the premillennial form of dispensationalists in regard to Israel, and the conversion to Christianity of 144,000 Jewish evangelists that is expected in the last days, see also the dozen *Left Behind* novels by Tim LaHaye and Jerry B. Jenkins (Wheaton, Ill.: Tyndale House Publishers) that have sold fifty million copies in the United States.

25. All quotes from February 28, 2003, editions, following George W. Bush's speech on Feburary 27 giving the president's imprimatur to the Wilsonian war aim of democratic transformation in the Mideast, by the sword, if necessary.

26. See, for example, Steinbach, "The Iraqi Fata Morgana."

27. Interviews with U.S. ambassador to Germany Daniel Coats and other senior American and German officials. For a more thorough treatment of this dispute, see Stephen Szabo, "A Poisoned Victory? German-American Relations and the Election of 2002," in David P. Conradt and others, eds., *A Precarious Victory: Schroeder and the German Elections of 2002* (manuscript). For an account of the "isolated Germans" and "indifferent Americans" in the heat of battle by a veteran German defender of America, see Josef Joffe, "Die grosse Entfremdung" (The great alienation), *Die Zeit*, September 5, 2002, p. 1. For Ambassador Coats's evaluation of German-American relations, see Thomas Hanke, "Coats rechnet mit Neubewertung der Beziehungen" (Coats counts on a revaluation of relations), *Financial Times Deutschland*, March 17, 2003, p. 16.

28. For Klose's criticism of Schröder's course, see Hans-Ulrich Klose, "In der Abseitsfalle" (In the trap of being shunted aside), *Frankfurter Allgemeine Zeitung*, February 14, 2003, p. 31.

29. A personal anecdote captures the mood here. A German acquaintance I had not seen for four years tracked down my new telephone number in Berlin, called me to express her distress, and said that her mother was sitting at home in front

of the TV weeping, because—in reference to American help for Germany when Schröder grew up in a poor single-parent family after World War II—"If it weren't for the Americans, Schröder wouldn't even be here!"

30. E. J. Dionne, "A Double Standard on Dissent," *Washington Post*, March 21, 2003, p. A37.

31. Woodward, *Bush at War*, p. 277.

32. John Lewis Gaddis, "A Grand Strategy," *Foreign Policy*, no. 133 (November/December 2002), pp. 50–57. For a positive German Christian Democratic evaluation of the strategy, see Karl-Heinz Kamp, "Prevention in US Security Strategy," *Transatlantic Internationale Politik*, vol. 4, no. 1 (Spring 2003), pp. 17–20. For reportage stressing the American warning that if NATO is to remain relevant, it must radically change its structures and doctrines so it can operate at any time in any theater, see Judy Dempsey, "NATO Challenged to Make Radical Shift in Principles and Practice," *Financial Times*, September 21, 2002, p 9. For a Council on Foreign Relations study postulating that the strategy statement was still subject to implementation in either traditional or hard-line forms, see Lawrence J. Korb, *A New National Security Strategy in an Age of Terrorists, Tyrants, and Weapons of Mass Destruction: Three Options Presented as Presidential Speeches* (New York: Council on Foreign Relations, 2003).

33. Conversation with the author, June 2003. A senior German diplomat suggested that the question of whether the notion of preventive war would become a bone of transatlantic contention would depend entirely on the case-by-case application of it. Author's interview, October 2002.

34. For an enthusiastic German presentation of the oil-explains-everything thesis, see *Der Spiegel*'s cover story on January 13, 2003, "Blut für Öl: Worum es in Irak wirklich geht" (Blood for oil: What it's really all about in Iraq), pp. 94–109. For a German refutation of this thesis in the same week, see the full-page interview with economist William D. Hordhaus, "Ein Krieg ums Öl ist ökonomischer Unsinn" (A war for oil is economic nonsense), *Die Zeit*, January 16, 2003, p. 17.

35. For the continuing postwar debate about development of low-yield nuclear "bunker busters," with American neoconservative fans of the weapon pitted against appalled Europeans, see Michael A. Levi, "A Nuclear Option That America Does Not Need," *Financial Times*, August 15, 2003; and William J. Broad, "Facing a Second Nuclear Age," *New York Times*, August 3, 2003.

36. Analyzing output rather than intent, Carnegie Endowment researchers found the U.S. performance unimpressive in trying to build democracy elsewhere under any conditions remotely resembling those in Iraq. Out of sixteen attempts in the past century, only four established democracy that lasted ten years or more—in the ministates of Grenada and Panama and in the two countries that surrendered unconditionally in World War II, Germany and Japan. Minxin Pei and Sara Kasper, "Lessons from the Past: The American Record in Nation Building" (Washington: Carnegie Endowment, April 2003).

37. See http://usinfo.state.gov/topical/pol/terror/02110803.htm.

38. For a positive European evaluation of the NRF, see Alyson J. K. Bailes,

"NATO's New Response Force," *Transatlantic Internationale Politik,* vol. 4, no. 1 (Spring 2003), pp. 25–29.

39. Many veteran political observers in Berlin, including Schröder's longtime political foe, deputy Union caucus leader Wolfgang Schäuble, doubt that Schröder would have remained as adamant as he did on the Iraq issue after the election if Bush had not rebuffed all gestures of reconciliation and continued to isolate him. Interview with Schäuble, June 2003.

40. For good overviews of French-German relations just before the anniversary, see Robert Graham and Haig Simonian, "After 40 Years Together, France and Germany May Be Struggling to Keep the Spark in Their Close Relationship," *Financial Times,* January 20, 2003, p. 11; and Karl Kaiser and others, "*Deutschland, Frankreich und Europa: Perspektiven*" (Germany, France, and Europe: Prospects), DGAP-Analyse Nr. 21 (German Council on Foreign Relations and the French Institute of Foreign Relations [IFRI], January 2003), 21 pp.

41. Conversation with the author, February 2003.

42. On Germany's quiet provision of AWACS surveillance and Patriots to Turkey, see, for example, Christian Wernicke and Christoph Schwennicke, "Bundeswehr muss mit grösserem Türkei-Einsatz rechnen" (Bundeswehr must count on larger operation in Turkey), *Süddeutsche Zeitung,* February 20, 2003, p. 1; and Awacs-Besatzungen bleiben vorläufig im Einsatz" (AWACS crews remain in operation for now), *Frankfurter Allgemeine Zeitung,* March 24, 2003, p. 1.

43. For one detailed account of this row, see James Kitfield, "Damage Control," *National Journal,* July 19, 2003, as carried in the NATO Enlargement Daily Brief—Op/Eds of July 18, 2003, archived at http://groups.yahoo.com/group/nedb/messages. This account, like most American and British media coverage, treats the NATO spat as "the perfect storm," that is, an accidental "rare confluence of opposing currents in international affairs, bad political timing, and questionable political leadership" that whipped out of anyone's control. The view of this book, by contrast, is that the clash was a deliberate and real test of the new hegemonic style of the United States.

44. See, for example, Stefan Kornelius, "Doppelte Eindämmung" (Double containment), *Süddeutsche Zeitung,* February 14, 2003.

45. "Blix speaks—and the Stakes Could Not Be Higher for the Transatlantic Allies Bitterly Divided over War with Iraq," *Financial Times,* February 14, 2003, p. 11.

46. Philip Stephens, "The Transatlantic Alliance Is Worse Off than the Coalition," *Financial Times,* March 28, 2003, p. 15.

47. "Den Krieg aufhalten" ("Stop the war"), *Süddeutsche Zeitung,* February 14, 2003, p. 4.

48. For the unfortunate consequences in Turkey, see Leyla Boulton, "A Hopeful Picture Turned on Its Head," *Financial Times,* April 1, 2003, special section; and her earlier "Ankara Goes to the Wire over US Aid for Supporting War," *Financial Times,* February 20, 2003, p. 3.

49. Ivo Daalder, "Bush's Coalition Doesn't Add Up Where It Counts," *Newsday,* March 24, 2003.

50. Quoted in Philip Stephens, "Bush and Blair's differing designs for a secure world," *Financial Times*, March 21, 2003, p. 16. For one sample of the flurry of alarmed think-tank pleas for transatlantic solidarity by elites in May, after the announced close of major hostilities in Iraq on May 1, see "Joint Declaration on Renewing the Transatlantic Partnership," signed by Madeleine Albright, Zbigniew Brzezinski, and others, prepared by Simon Serfaty at the Center for Strategic and International Studies, http://csis.org.Europe/2003_May_14JointDeclr.pdf.

Chapter Four

1. See Max Boot, "The New American Way of War," *Foreign Affairs*, vol. 82, no. 4 (July/August 2003), pp. 41–58; and Richard Perle, "Lessons of Operation Iraqi Freedom," AEI Online, posted August 11, 2003, www.aei.org/publications/pubID.19017/pub_detail.asp. For a less partisan analysis of the military campaign in Iraq, see Timothy Garden, "Iraq: The Military Campaign," *International Affairs*, vol. 79, no. 4 (July 2003), pp. 701–18. See also the transcript of the April 15 black-coffee briefing at the American Enterprise Institute, available at www.aei.org/events/eventID.273/transcript.asp.

2. Jimmy Burns, "US Told Stance May Spur Anarchy in Iraq," *Financial Times*, July 11, 2003, p. 1; "Walking on Eggshells," *Economist*, July 5, 2003, p. 1.

3. According to Jordan's Prince El Hassan Bin Talal at the June 18–20 World Forum conference in Brussels on National Sovereignty and Universal Challenges: Choices for the World after Iraq. "Conference Report" (European Centre for Public Affairs, July 4, 2003).

4. Jessica Stern, "How America Created a Terrorist Haven," *New York Times*, August 20, 2003. See also Neil MacFarquhar, "Rising Tide of Islamic Militants See Iraq as Ultimate Battlefield," *New York Times*, August 13, 2003.

5. See, for example, James Risen, "U.S. Asks Ex-U.N. Inspector to Advise on Arms Search for Bush," *New York Times*, June 12, 2003; Douglas Jehl, "Iraqi Trailers Said to Make Hydrogen, Not Biological Arms," *New York Times*, August 9, 2003; and the Council on Foreign Relations Q&A on WMD, accessible at www.cfr.org.

6. James Blitz and James Harding, "Blair Should Quit, Half the British Public Believe," *Financial Times*, September 27, 2003; and Robert Worcester, "Blair Sees Popularity Fall," *Financial Times*, September 8, 2003, p. 3. Spanish prime minister Aznar faced the same charge that he had exaggerated the Iraqi WMD threat. "Aznar's Mühen mit der Kriegspropaganda" (Aznar's trouble with war propaganda), *Neue Zürcher Zeitung*, August 13, 2003.

7. See Walter Pincus, "Report Cast Doubt on Iraq–Al Qaeda Connection," *Washington Post*, June 22, 2003, p. A1.

8. David Broder, "Black Thursday," *Washington Post*, July 15, 2003, p. A19.

9. "Nur jeder zweite Amerikaner glaubt seinem Präsidenten" (Only every other American believes his president), *Neue Zürcher Zeitung*, July 31, 2003, citing NBC and *Wall Street Journal* polls that showed 47 percent thought he had exaggerated, 48 percent thought he adhered to facts.

10. Thom Shanker, "New Top General Tells Legislators U.S. Will Probably Need a Larger Army," *New York Times*, July 30, 2003.

11. Jessica Stern, "The Protean Enemy," *Foreign Affairs*, vol. 82, no. 4 (July/August 2003), pp. 27–40; Martin Wagener, "Al Qaeda in Southeast Asia," *Transatlantic Internationale Politik*, vol. 4, no. 2 (Summer 2003), pp. 85–90; and Angel M. Rabasa, "Political Islam in Southeast Asia: Moderates, Radicals and Terrorists," Adelphi Paper 358 (London: International Institute for Strategic Studies, May 2003).

12. For one plea for European acquisition of net-centric force multipliers that could retrofit EU countries' twentieth-century weapons for twenty-first century wars, see Klaus Naumann, "NATO and the EU's Strategic Choices, *Transatlantic Internationale Politik*, vol. 4, no. 3 (Fall 2003), pp. 11–16.

13. "What's Next? Preserving American Primacy, Institutionalizing Unipolarity," May 1, 2003, www.aei.org/publications/pubID.16999/pub_detail.asp. Contrast this optimistic American view about the consequences of victory in Iraq with the gloomy European view of Anatol Lieven, a British expatriate in Washington and a journalist with special expertise in former Soviet lands. Lieven sees the more likely result of the clash between the "dangerous phenomenon" of "wounded nationalism" in the United States and Arab humiliation as a rapid increase in recruitment of terrorists. "The danger is not so much that the Bush administration will consciously adopt the whole Neo-Con imperialist programme as that the Neo-Cons and their allies will contribute to tendencies stemming inexorably from the US occupation of Iraq and that the result will be a vicious circle of terrorism and war. If this proves to be the case, then the damage inflicted over time by the US on the Muslim world and by Muslims on the US and its allies is likely to be horrendous," he wrote in "A Trap of Their Own Making," *London Review of Books*, vol. 25, no. 9 (May 8, 2003), accessible at www.ceip.org.

14. There were some signs that such a shift did occur in the German weekly magazines. As the Iraq war began, *Stern* and *Der Spiegel*—their cover stories were headlined "Bombenterror für die Freiheit: Amerikas Krieg gegen Saddam" (Bombterror for freedom: America's war against Saddam), *Der Spiegel*, March 24, 2003, and "Bush Spiel mit dem Feuer: Krieg im Namen der Freiheit" (Bush plays with fire: war in the name of freedom), *Stern*, March 20, 2003—exulted in German emancipation from the United States, asked if "Bush's war" would set the entire world ablaze, and featured coverage of the increase in cancer and deformities in Iraqi children from American uranium ammunition used in the Gulf War. By contrast, after the war *Der Spiegel* ran a cover story on "The murder clan" of Saddam Hussein ("Der Mörder-Clan," June 16, 2003), while *Stern* blandly displayed a blonde with the characteristic S-shaped universal tool for its cover story "IKEA: wie der Möbelgigant wirklich funktioniert" (IKEA: how the furniture giant really works), April 24, 2003. Most remarkably, perhaps, later in the summer *Stern* self-mockingly referred to Germany as "Pacifistan" (July 11, 2003).

15. See, for example, Max Boot, "POWER: Resentment Comes with the Territory," *Washington Post*, March 23, 2003, p. B1.

16. "We must have no illusions," wrote that long-time friend of America Pierre Hassner in April 2003: "The United States, after having supported European unity, and then having had doubts about it, is now doing everything to divide the Europeans. That is yet another reason not to play their game." Pierre Hassner, "War: Who Is to Blame?" *Centre for European Reform Bulletin*, vol. 29 (April/May 2003), pp. 2ff.

17. Author's conversation with Norbert Walter, head of research at Deutsche Bank, May 2003. Given the thorough mix of nationalities working for all major banks, Deutsche Bank simply had its most recently acquired American executive call some of his old colleagues to get the information anyway.

18. Blair speech in parliament, March 18, 2003, www.number-10.gov.uk/output/Page3294.asp; "Why Blair Fears America," *Economist*, March 22, 2003, p. 40; Philip Stephens, "Blair Will Emerge as a Stronger and Wiser Leader," *Financial Times*, March 24, 2003, p. 15; and author's background interviews.

19. Presidency Conclusions, Brussels European Council, March 20–21, 2003, http://ue.eu.int/pressData/en/ec/75136.pdf.

20. "Embittered Partners Look for a Reason to Believe in Reconciliation" and "Chirac Plans to Resist the Control of Postwar Iraq by US Allies," both in *Financial Times*, March 22, 2003, p. 6; "Debating How to Put Iraq Back Together Again," *Financial Times*, March 22, 2003, p. 9; "Remaking the World after the Iraq War," *Financial Times*, March 21, 2003, p. 14; "Deutschland bereitet Wiederaufbau Iraks vor" (Germany makes preparations for Iraq's reconstruction), *Financial Times Deutschland*, March 17, 2003, p. 16; "Die Ausputztruppe" (The cleanup troops), *Die Zeit*, March 20, 2003, p. 10; "Chirac Expresses Regret but Offers to Help Rebuild," *Financial Times*, March 21, p. 2; "Chirac Says Rebuilding of Iraq Must Be U.N. Job," *Wall Street Journal Europe*, March 24, 2003; and author's background interviews.

21. "Blair's Address to a Joint Session of Congress," *New York Times*, July 17, 2003.

22. "US Policy and the Israeli-Palestinian Dispute/Re-engagement after Iraq?" IISS *Strategic Comments*, vol. 9, no. 2 (March 2003).

23. See David Schoenbaum, *The United States and the State of Israel* (Oxford University Press, 1993).

24. Author's conversation with Solana, March 2003.

25. Philip Stephens, "The World's Hyperpower Unrivalled but Vulnerable," *Financial Times*, September 26, 2003, p. 15. See also "Crisis in Palestine," *IISS Strategic Comments* 9, no. 7 (London: October 1, 2003).

26. Author's conversation with EU official, September 2003.

27. See www.usinfo.pl/bushvisit/2003.

28. See also Elizabeth Becker, "U.S. Plans to Run Iraq Itself," *New York Times*, March 25, 2003.

29. "Berlin fühlt sich von Polen übergangen" (Berlin feels Poland went behind its back), *Neue Zürcher Zeitung*, May 8, 2003.

30. A CBOS survey at the end of July showed that only 36 percent of Poles

favored sending troops to Iraq as against 55 percent opposed. This was a turn-around from the 50 percent pro and 33 percent con of the previous month. Tom Hundley, "Poles Getting Cold Feet over Combat Mission / Populace Wary about Peacekeeping Duties," *Star-Ledger*, August 4, 2003, carried in NATO Enlargement Daily Brief, August 5, 2003, archived at http://groups.yahoo.com/group/nedb/messages.

31. Reuters, "Bush Dines with Iraq War Opponents, Greets Schröder," May 31, 2003.

32. See Gunter Hofmann, "Im Einklang mit dem Rest der Welt" (In harmony with the rest of the world), *Die Zeit*, April 10, 2003, p. 8; and Nico Fried, "Europas Kernchen" (Europe's teeny core), *Süddeutsche Zeitung*, April 23, 2003, p. 4.

33. Michael Gonzalez, "Selling the Atlantic," *Wall Street Journal Europe*, May 7, 2003. For German commentary ridiculing any European "defense union" that excludes the British or fails to share America's global burdens, see Michael Stürmer, "Half Farce und half Tragödie" (Half farce and half tragedy), *Die Welt*, April 29, 2003. See also Cornelia Bolesch, "Pralinen, schlecht verpackt/Der Brüsseler Mini-Gipfel zur Verteidigungspolitik hat die richtigen Ideen falsch inszeniert" (Pralines badly packaged/The Brussels minisummit on security policy has the right ideas staged wrongly), *Süddeutsche Zeitung*, April 30, 2003, p. 4; Klaus-Dieter Frankenberger, "Verdacht" (Suspicion), *Frankfurter Allgemeine Zeitung*, April 29, 2003, p. 1; Horst Bacia, "Unnötige Eile" (Unnecessary haste), *Frankfurter Allgemeine Zeitung*, April 28, 2003, p. 12; and Stefan Kornelius, "Lektion in Realpolitik" (Lesson in realpolitik), *Süddeutsche Zeitung*, April 28, 2003, p. 4.

34. Speech at the Atlantic Council's "Salute to the New NATO," in Washington on May 5, 2003; distributed by NATO.

35. "A Secure Europe in a Better World," June 19/20, 2003, http://ue.eu.int. For a German analysis of the document, see Eckart Lohse, "Wieder Anschluss an Amerika finden" (To reconnect with America), *Frankfurter Allgemeine Zeitung*, June 21, 2003, p. 3.

36. For different takes on NATO's dilemmas and options, see Christopher Coker, "Globalisation and Insecurity in the Twenty-First Century: NATO and the Management of Risk," Adelphi Paper 345 (London: International Institute for Strategic Studies, June 2002); Lothar Rühl, "Vorwärtsverteidigung und globale Ordnung" (Forward defense and global order), *Neue Zürcher Zeitung*, August 9, 2003, p. 4; and Thomas Donnelly, "Rethinking NATO," *NATO Review*, June 1, 2003, www.aei.org/news/newsID.18924/news_detail.asp.

37. See, for example, Jan Ross, "Wer einmal lügt . . ." (He who lies once . . .), *Die Zeit*, July 24, 2003, p. 1; Reiner Luyken, "Der Entzauberte" (The disenchanted), *Die Zeit*, July 31, 2003, p. 9; and James Harding, "Bush Faces Growing Scrutiny on Iraq 'Threat,'" *Financial Times*, August 11, 2003, p. 4.

38. Charles Kupchan, *The End of the American Era: U.S. Foreign Policy after the Cold War* (Alfred Knopf, 2002).

39. See, for example, Klaus Naumann, "NATO and the EU's Strategic Choices," *Transatlantic Internationale Politik*, vol. 4, no. 3 (Fall 2003), pp. 11–16; and Thomas

Risse, "For a New Transatlantic—and European—Bargain," *Transatlantic Internationale Politik*, vol. 4, no. 3 (Fall 2003), pp. 20–28.

40. Heinrich Vogel, "The End of the 'Old West,'" *Transatlantic Internationale Politik*, vol. 4, no. 3 (Fall 2003), pp. 15–19.

41. World Forum, "Conference Report." For a more vitriolic expression of revulsion at Bush administration leadership, see Denis Duclos, "Délires paranöiaques et culture de la haine en Amérique" (Paranoiac delusions and the culture of hate in America) *Le Monde Diplomatique*, August 2003, pp. 12ff.

42. Conversation with the author, June 2003. For sympathetic summaries of the evolution of the Common Foreign and Security Policy (CFSP) and the European Security and Defense Policy (ESDP), including the important preparation of police cadres for foreign peacekeeping missions, see Brian Crowe, "A Common European Foreign Policy after Iraq?" *International Affairs*, vol. 79, no. 3 (May 2003), pp. 533–46; Roy Ginsberg, *The European Union in International Politics* (Lanham, Md.: Rowman & Littlefield, 2001); Roy H. Ginsberg, "Ten Years of European Union Foreign Policy: Baptism, Confirmation, Validation" (Washington: Heinrich Böll Foundation, 2002), 40 pp., and Esther Brimmer, ed., *The EU's Search for a Strategic Role* (Washington: Center for Transatlantic Relations, 2003).

43. On consensus between old and new Europeans see, for example, Adam Krzeminski, "Poland's Home Is Europe," *Transatlantic Internationale Politik*, vol. 4, no. 3 (Fall 2003), pp. 65–68; Quentin Peel, "A Strong Penchant for Old Europe," *Financial Times*, August 12, 2003, p. 11; and "Irak-Discussionen in Budapest und Kiew" (Iraq discussion in Budapest and Kyiv), *Neue Zürcher Zeitung*, August 9, 2003, p. 3. On a new understanding in international law of when foreign intervention is justified, see S. Neil MacFarlane, "Intervention in Contemporary World Politics," Adelphi Paper 350 (London: International Institute for Strategic Studies, August 2002).

44. "America's Image Further Erodes, Europeans Want Weaker Ties," opinion survey released March 18, 2001, by the Pew Research Center for the People and the Press, http://people-press.org/reports/display.php3?ReportID=175.

45. George Melloan, "Germany Makes a Choice, and It Isn't France," *Wall Street Journal*, July 22, 2003, as carried in the U.S. Latvian Embassy NATO Enlargement Daily Brief Op-Eds, July 22, 2003, archived at http://groups.yahoo.com/group/nedb/messages. See also Frederick Kempe and Marc Champion, "In a Shift, Schröder Says Germany Is Ready to Help U.S. Rebuild Iraq," *Wall Street Journal*, September 18, 2003, p. 1. The friendly tone of Melloan's article (except toward France) contrasted sharply with the chip-on-the-shoulder tone of much of the conservative American commentary about Europeans in March, April, and May. See, for example, David Frum, "Blair Must Find the Courage to Turn His Back on the EU," *Daily Telegraph* (London), March 24, 2003, www.aei.org/news/newsID.16683/news_detail.asp; and Michael A. Ledeen, "The Crucible of Leadership," *Jerusalem Post*, March 21, 2003, www.aei.org/news/newsID.16685/news_detail.asp. For the quite different European take on the bilateral rap-

prochement and meeting that regarded Bush as having moderated his tone rather more than Schröder, see Hugh Williamson, "Schröder and Bush Hold Talks to Ease Tensions," *Financial Times*, September 24, 2003. p. 3; "Reparatur" (Repair), *Frankfurter Allgemeine Zeitung*, September 24, 2003, p. 10; "Streit in Aller Freundschaft" (Quarrel in all friendliness), *Süddeutsche Zeitung*, September 24, 2003, p. 4; and Kurt Kister, "Und er nennt ihn wieder Görard" (And he calls him Görard again), *Süddeutsche Zeitung*, September 25, 2003, p. 3. For an acid call for Europe's "emancipation from U.S. tutelage," see Heinrich Jaenecke, "Die Stune der Wahrheit" (The moment of truth), *Stern*, September 18, 2003, pp. 36ff.

46. The rise and fall of European hopes for a transatlantic reconciliation were reflected in the shift of German and Swiss headlines from August 11 to 19: "Bush sucht Partner für Aufbau im Irak" (Bush seeks partners for reconstruction in Iraq), *Süddeutsche Zeitung*, August 11, 2003, p. 1; "Bush lobt Schröder, weil er ihn braucht" (Bush praises Schröder because he needs him), *Süddeutsche Zeitung*, August 11, 2003, p. 4; "Berlin befürwortet Nato-Einsatz im Irak/Die Bundesregierung erfreut über Präsident Bushs Lob" (Berlin approves NATO operation in Iraq/Government happy about President Bush's praise), *Neue Zürcher Zeitung*, August 11, 2003, p. 1; Christian Wernicke, "Gestern Kampfanzug, heute Zwangsjacke/Die USA benutzen die Nato, um Europas Sicherheitspolitik weiter zu kontrollieren" (Yesterday a uniform, today a straitjacket/The USA uses NATO to continue controlling Europe's security policy), *Süddeutsche Zeitung*, August 19, 2003; Nico Fried, "Berlin schließt deutsche Beteiligung im Irak aus" (Berlin excludes German participation in Iraq), *Süddeutsche Zeitung*, August 19, 2003. For a more general discussion of the European viewpoint on peacekeeping in Iraq, see Jeremy Smith, "EU Might Not Fund Iraq Aid if War Illegal: Patten," Reuters, March 12, 2003; and Martin Wolf, "Supremacy Is Not Enough to Remake the World Order," *Financial Times*, July 9, 2003, p. 13. For the neoconservative insistence on total U.S. control in postwar Iraq, see Reuel Marc Gerecht, "Help Not Wanted," *Weekly Standard*, August 18, 2003, www.aei.org/news/newsID.19007/news_detail.asp. See also Robert Gerald Livingston, "Patching Up German-American Relations," *Transatlantic Internationale Politik* vol. 4, no. 3 (Fall 2003), pp. 49–56; James Kitfield, "NATO Could Help in Iraq, but Will It?" *National Journal*, vol. 26, July 26, 2003, carried in NATO Enlargement Daily Brief, July 25, 2003, archived at http://groups.yahoo.com/group/nedb; and Max Boot, "America and the U.N., Together Again?" *New York Times*, August 3, 2003.

47. German Marshall Fund of the U.S./Compagnia di San Paolo, *Transatlantic Trends 2003*, released in September 2003, www.transatlantictrends.org; Pew Research Center for the People and the Press, *Views of a Changing World, June 2003*, www.people-press.org; Peter Slevin, "Changes in U.S. Diplomacy Sought," *Washington Post*, October 2, 2003, p. A16.

48. Lael Brainard and Michael O'Hanlon "The Heavy Price of America's Going It Alone," *Financial Times*, August 6, 2003, p. 13.

49. Other pollsters cited here include John Zogby, NBC/*Wall Street Journal*, and the University of Maryland's Program on International Policy. See Robert Dallek,

"Patience May Not Be an Option," *Washington Post*, September 28, 2003, p. B1; Edward Alden, "US Stance 'Making Terrorism More Likely,'" *Financial Times*, September 10, 2003, p. 2; Mark Huband and others, "The West Has Hit al-Qaeda Hard but Terrorism Is Still a Formidable Enemy," *Financial Times*, September 11, 2003; and Martin Wolf, "Funding America's Recovery Is a Very Dangerous Game," *Financial Times*, October 1, 2003, p. 13.

50. Edward Alden, "US 'Had No New Evidence of WMD' in Iraq," *Financial Times*, September 29, 2003, p. 4.

51. See especially Senator Joseph Biden, "The National Dialogue on Iraq + One Year," speech at the Brookings Institution, July 31, 2003, www.brookings.edu/comm/events/20030731.htm; Zbigniew Brzezinski, "Where Do We Go from Here?" *Transatlantic Internationale Politik,* vol. 4, no. 3 (Fall 2003), pp. 3–10; Madeleine K. Albright, "Bridges, Bombs, or Bluster?" *Foreign Affairs*, vol. 82, no. 5 (September/October 2003), pp. 2–19; and Ronals Asmus and Kenneth Pollack, "The Neoliberal Take on the Middle East," *Washington Post*, July 22, 2003.

52. Paul Kennedy, "The Perils of Empire," *Washington Post*, April 20, 2003, p. B1.

53. Guy Dinmore, "Cracks Appear in America's Neo-conservative Consensus," *Financial Times*, September 23, 2003, p. 16.

54. See Carl Hulse and David E. Sanger, "New Criticism on Prewar Use of Intelligence," *New York Times*, September 29, 2003.

55. Dean Acheson, *Present at the Creation* (W. W. Norton, 1987 reissue), p. 729.

Persons Interviewed

Benoit d'Aboville, French ambassador to Poland; later, French ambassador to the
North Atlantic Treaty Organization (NATO)

Rudolf Adam, vice president, German Intelligence Service

Günther Altenburg, NATO assistant secretary general for political affairs

Walter Andrusyszyn, European desk, U.S. National Security Council

Paddy Ashdown, international high representative in Bosnia-Herzegovina

Shlomo Avineri, professor, The Hebrew University of Jerusalem; former general
director of Israel's Foreign Ministry

Christoph Bertram, director, German Institute for International and Security
Affairs, Berlin

Hans-Henning Blomeyer-Bartenstein, deputy national security adviser to the German
chancellor

Michael Broer, German Defense Ministry

Ekkehard Brose, head of Defense and Security Policy Division, German Foreign
Ministry

Günter Burkhardt, ambassador, Delegation of the European Commission in
Washington

Nicholas Burns, U.S. ambassador to NATO

Andrzej Byrt, Polish ambassador to Germany

Jürgen Chrobog, state secretary, German Foreign Ministry

Daniel R. Coats, U.S. ambassador to Germany

Robert Cooper, adviser to EU high representative for foreign policy Javier Solana

Jeremy Cresswell, deputy head of the British mission, Berlin

Nikolaos van Dam, Netherlands ambassador to Germany

Jonathan Davidson, senior advisor, political and academic affairs, delegation of the
European Commission in Washington

Chris Donnelly, special adviser to NATO secretary general for Central and East
European affairs

Willem van Eekelen, former secretary-general, Western European Union

Gernot Erler, deputy head of the Social Democratic parliamentary caucus and SPD spokesman for foreign policy

Isabelle François, staff officer, Defense Partnership and Cooperation Directorate, NATO

Daniel Fried, senior director for European affairs, U.S. National Security Council

Philip H. Gordon, Director of the Center on the United States and France and senior fellow at the Brookings Institution

Przemyslaw Grudzinski, Polish ambassador to the United States

Michael Haltzel, senior professional staff member, Committee on Foreign Relations, U.S. Senate

Daniel Hamilton, director, Center for Transatlantic Relations, Washington

Danuta Hübner, Polish European Integration minister

Robert Hunter, RAND, Washington; former U.S. ambassador to NATO

Wolfgang Ischinger, German ambassador to the United States

Jackson Janes, director, American Institute for Contemporary German Studies, Washington

Karl Kaiser, director of studies, German Council on Foreign Relations

Dieter Kastrup, National Security Adviser to the German Chancellor

Jacques Paul Klein, special representative of the UN secretary-general in Bosnia and Herzegovina

Hans-Ulrich Klose, Social Democratic member of the Bundestag

Eberhard Kölsch, deputy head of the German mission, Washington

John Kornblum, Berlin chairman, Lazard & Co. Investment Banking, Berlin; former U.S. ambassador to Germany

Harald Kujat, chairman of NATO's Military Committee

Philippe Lalliot, counselor, French embassy, Washington

Sir Paul Lever, British ambassador to Germany

Claude Martin, French ambassador to Germany

Michael Mertes, consultant in Bonn, former domestic adviser to Chancellor Helmut Kohl

Bowman Miller, director, Office of Analysis for Europe and Canada, Bureau of Intelligence and Research, U.S. State Department

Gebhardt von Moltke, German ambassador to NATO

Ursula Müller, political counselor, German Embassy in Washington

William Nash, Council on Foreign Relations, Washington

Klaus Naumann, retired general, former chairman of NATO's Military Committee

Michael O'Neill, British embassy, Washington

Janusz Onyszkiewicz, Center for International Relations, Warsaw, former Polish minister of defense

Steve Orosz, director, Civil Emergency Planning, NATO

Günter Pleuger, German ambassador to the United Nations

Pamela Quanrud, Head of EU desk, U.S. National Security Council

Adam Daniel Rotfeld, Polish deputy foreign minister

Michael Rühle, head of the policy planning and speechwriting section, NATO Political Affairs Division

Michael Schaefer, political director, German Foreign Ministry

Wolfgang Schäuble, deputy head of the CDU/CSU Bundestag caucus

Klaus Scharioth, state secretary, German Foreign Ministry

Jamie Shea, director, public affairs, NATO

Stanley Sloan, American consultant on NATO affairs

Hal Sonnenfeldt, guest scholar, Brookings Institution

Daniel Speckhard, deputy assistant secretary general for political affairs, NATO

Michael Steiner, chief of UN Mission in Kosovo; earlier, National Security Adviser to Chancellor Gerhard Schröder

Peter Struck, German defense minister

Walther Stützle, head of planning staff, German Defense Ministry

Steven Sturm, head of section, Defense Policy and Capabilities Directorate, NATO

Rita Süssmuth, former Speaker of the Bundestag

Horst Teltschik, board chairman, BMW Herbert Quandt Foundation; earlier, National Security Adviser to Chancellor Helmut Kohl

Roman Waschuk, counselor, Canadian embassy in Germany

E. A. Wayne, U.S. assistant secretary of state

David Wright, Canadian ambassador to NATO and dean of the NATO diplomatic corps

Suggestions for Further Reading

Books

Acheson, Dean. *Present at the Creation.* W. W. Norton, 1987 reissue.

Allemann, Fritz René. *Bonn Ist Nicht Weimar* (Bonn is not Weimar). Cologne: Kiepenheuer & Witsch, reissued in 2000 in Frankfurt by R. G. Fischer.

Berman, Paul. *Terror and Liberalism.* W. W. Norton, 2003.

Bielka, Frauke N., and Christian Tuschoff. "Common Threats—Diverging Responses." Washington: American Institute for Contemporary German Studies, April 2001.

Brimmer, Esther, ed. *The EU's Search for a Strategic Role* (Washington: Center for Transatlantic Relations, 2003).

Coker, Christopher. "Globalisation and Insecurity in the Twenty-First Century: NATO and the Management of Risk." Adelphi Paper 345. London: International Institute for Strategic Studies, June 2002.

Cooper, Robert. *The Post-Modern State and the World Order.* London: Demos, 1996.

Dobbins, James, and others. *America's Role in Nation-Building from Germany to Iraq* (Washington: RAND, 2003).

Dodge, Toby. *Inventing Iraq: The Failure of Nation Building and a History Denied* (Columbia University Press, 2003).

Doyle, Michael. *Ways of War and Peace.* W. W. Norton, 1997.

Freedman, Lawrence, ed., *Superterrorism: Policy Responses.* Oxford: Blackwell, 2002.

Frum, David. *The Right Man.* Random House, 2003.

Fukuyama, Francis. *The End of History and the Last Man.* Free Press, 1992.

Ginsberg, Roy. *The European Union in International Politics.* Lanham, Md.: Rowman & Littlefield, 2001.

Grant, Charles. *Transatlantic Rift: How to Bring the Two Sides Together* (London: Centre for European Reform, 2003).

Hirschman, Albert O. *Exit, Voice, and Loyalty.* Harvard University Press, 1970.

Howard, Michael. *The Invention of Peace.* Yale University Press, 2000.

Huntington, Samuel. *The Clash of Civilizations and the Remaking of World Order.* Touchstone, 1988.

Hutton, Will. *The World We're In.* London: Little, Brown, 2002.

Ikenberry, G. John. *After Victory.* Princeton University Press, 2001.

International Institute for Strategic Studies. *Strategic Survey 2002/3.* London: 2003.

Kagan, Robert. *Of Paradise and Power.* Knopf, 2003.

Kaplan, Lawrence F., and William Kristol. *The War over Iraq.* San Francisco: Encounter, 2003.

Kennedy, Paul. *The Rise and Fall of the Great Powers.* Random House, 1987.

Korb, Lawrence J. *A New National Security Strategy in an Age of Terrorists, Tyrants, and Weapons of Mass Destruction: Three Options Presented as Presidential Speeches.* New York: Council on Foreign Relations, 2003.

Kupchan, Charles. *The End of the American Era: U.S. Foreign Policy after the Cold War.* Knopf, 2002.

Lipset, Seymour Martin. *American Exceptionalism.* W. W. Norton, 1996.

MacFarlane, S. Neil. "Intervention in Contemporary World Politics." Adelphi Paper 350. London: International Institute for Strategic Studies, August 2002.

Mandelbaum, Michael. *The Dawn of Peace in Europe.* New York: Twentieth Century Fund Press, 1996.

———. *The Ideas That Conquered the World: Peace, Democracy, and Free Markets in the Twenty-First Century.* New York: Public Affairs, 2002.

Mead, Walter Russell. *Special Providence: American Foreign Policy and How It Changed the World.* New York: Century Foundation Book, 2002.

Mueller, John. *Retreat from Doomsday: The Obsolescence of Major War.* Basic Books, 1989.

Nye, Joseph S., Jr. *Bound to Lead.* Basic Books, 1990.

———. *The Paradox of American Power.* Oxford University Press, 2002.

Occhipinti, John D. *The Politics of EU Police Cooperation.* Boulder, Colo.: Lynne Rienner, 2003.

Pond, Elizabeth. *Beyond the Wall.* Brookings, 1993.

———. *The Rebirth of Europe.* Brookings, 2002, revised edition.

Prestowitz, Clyde. *Rogue Nation: American Unilateralism and the Failure of Good Intentions.* Basic Books, 2003.

Schäuble, Wolfgang. *Scheitert der Westen?* (Will the West fail?) (Gütersloh: Bertelsmann, 2003).

Schoenbaum, David. *The United States and the State of Israel.* Oxford University Press, 1993.

Szabo, Stephen. "A Poisoned Victory? German-American Relations and the Election of 2002." In *A Precarious Victory: Schroeder and the German Elections of 2002,* edited by David P. Conradt and others. Manuscript.

Weiler, J. H. H. *The Constitution of Europe.* Cambridge University Press, 1999.

Winkler, Heinrich August. *Der lange Weg nach Westen* (The long road to the West). Munich: Beck, 2000.

Woodward, Bob. *Bush at War*. Simon & Schuster, 2002.

Zelikow, Philip, and Condoleezza Rice. *Germany Unified and Europe Transformed*. Harvard University Press, 1997.

Speeches, Articles, and Essays

Albright, Madeleine K. "Bridges, Bombs, or Bluster?" *Foreign Affairs* 82, no. 5 (September/October 2003), pp. 2–19.

Allin, Dana H., and Steven Simon. "The Moral Psychology of US Support for Israel," *Survival* 45, no. 3 (Autumn 2003), pp. 123–44.

Bailes, Alyson J. K. "NATO's New Response Force." *Transatlantic Internationale Politik* 4, no. 1 (Spring 2003): 25–29.

Bertram, Christoph. "Shaping a Congenial Environment." *Survival* 44, no. 4 (Winter 2002/03): 139–45.

———. "Stärke und Schwäche (Strengths and weaknesses)." *Merkur* 57, no. 3 (March 2003): 200–06.

Biden, Joseph. "The National Dialogue on Iraq + One Year." Speech at the Brookings Institution, July 31, 2003, www.brookings.edu/comm/ events/20030731.htm.

Bielka, Frauke N., and Christian Tuschoff. "Common Threats—Diverging Responses." Washington: American Institute for Contemporary German Studies, April 2002.

Blair, Tony. "Blair's Address to a Joint Session of Congress." *New York Times*, July 18, 2003.

———. Speech in Parliament, March 18, 2003, www.number-10.gov.uk/output/Page3294.asp.

Boot, Max. "The New American Way of War." *Foreign Affairs* 82, no. 4 (July/August 2003): 41–58.

Brzezinski, Zbigniew. "Where Do We Go from Here?" *Transatlantic Internationale Politik* 4, no. 3 (Fall 2003), pp. 3–10.

Buruma, Ian. "How to Talk about Israel," *New York Times Magazine*, August 31, 2003.

Bush, George W. Address at West Point, June 1, 2002, www.whitehouse.gov/news/releases/2002/06/20020601-3.html.

———. Speech in Krakow, June 1, 2003, www.usinfo.pl/bushvisit/2003.

———. State of the Union address, January 29, 2002, www.whitehouse.gov/news/releases/2002/01/20020129-11.html.

Byman, Daniel L. "Building the New Iraq: The Role of Intervening Forces." *Survival* 45, no. 2 (Summer 2003): 57–71.

Carothers, Thomas. "Is Gradualism Possible? Choosing a Strategy for Promoting Democracy in the Middle East." Carnegie Endowment Working Paper 39 (June 2003).

Cheney, Dick. "Vice President Speaks at VFW 103rd National Convention," www.whitehouse.gov/news/releases/2002/08/20020826.html.

Chicago Council on Foreign Relations/German Marshall Fund of the US. "A World Transformed: Foreign Policy Attitudes of the U.S. Public after September 11," Sept. 4, 2002.

Cirincione, Joseph. "Origins of Regime Change in Iraq." Carnegie Proliferation Brief 6, no. 5 (March 19, 2003), www.ceip.org/files/nonprolif/ templates/Publicatons.asp?p=8&PublicationID=1214.

Clarke, Victoria. "The Christian Zionists." *Prospect* 88 (July 2003): 54–58.

Cooper, Robert. "How Shall We Answer Robert Kagan?" *Transatlantic Internationale Politik* 4, no. 2 (Summer 2003): 19–24.

Crowe, Brian. "A Common European Foreign Policy after Iraq?" *International Affairs* 79, no. 3 (May 2003): 533–46.

Daalder, Ivo. "The End of Atlanticism." *Survival* 45, no. 2 (Summer 2003): 147–65.

Dodge, Toby. "US Intervention and Possible Israeli Futures," *Survival* 45, no. 3 (Autumn 2003), 103–22.

Drew, Elizabeth. "The Neocons in Power." *New York Review of Books,* June 12, 2003.

European Council, Presidency Conclusions, Brussels European Council. March 20–21, 2003. http://europa.eu.int/newsroom/related.asp? BID=76&GRP= 5652&FROM=EuropeanCouncil_&LANG=1.

Everts, Steven. "Difficult but Necessary: A Transatlantic Strategy for the Greater Middle East." Paper presented at the German Marshall Fund Pre-[U.S.-EU] Summit Symposium, June 24, 2003.

Fukuyama, Francis. "Has History Restarted since September 11?" John Bonython Lecture at the Centre for Independent Studies. Melbourne, Australia, August 8, 2002.

Gaddis, John Lewis. "A Grand Strategy." *Foreign Policy* 133 (November/December 2002): 50–57.

Gargen, Timothy. "Iraq: the Military Campaign." *International Affairs* 79, no. 4 (July 2003): 701–18.

Garton Ash, Timothy. "Anti-Europeanism in America." *New York Review of Books,* March 27, 2003: 6–10.

Gingrich, Newt. "Rogue State Department." *Foreign Policy* 137 (July/August 2003): 42–49.

Gnesotto, Nicole. "Reacting to America." *Survival* 44, no. 4 (Winter 2002/03): 99–106.

Gordon, Philip H. "Bridging the Atlantic Divide." *Foreign Affairs* 82, no. 1 (January/February 2003): 70–83.

———. "Reforging the Atlantic Alliance." *National Interest* 69 (Fall 2002): 91–97.

Grant, Charles. "Powerless Europe." *Prospect,* March 2002.

Hamilton, Daniel. Testimony to the European Subcommittee of the House Committee on International Relations, June 11, 2003.

———. "Three Strategic Challenges for a Global Transatlantic Partnership." Paper presented at the German Marshall Fund Pre-[U.S.-EU] Summit Symposium, June 24, 2003. 11 pp.

Hamre, John, and others. "Iraq's Post-Conflict Reconstruction." Report commissioned by U.S. Defense Secretary Donald Rumsfeld, July 17, 2003, 10 pp., www.csis.org.

Hassner, Pierre. "Beyond the Three Traditions: The Philosophy of War and Peace in Historical Perspective." *International Affairs*, vol. 70, no. 4 (October 1994): 737–56.

———. *The United States: The Empire of Force or the Force of Empire?* Chaillot Paper 54. Paris: EU Institute for Security Studies, September 2002, www.iss-eu.org/.

Ikenberry, G. John. "America's Imperial Ambition." *Foreign Affairs* 81, no. 5 (September/October 2002): 44–60.

International Institute for Strategic Studies. "U.S. Policy and the Israeli-Palestinian Dispute/Re-engagement after Iraq?" *Strategic Comments* 9, no. 2 (March 2003).

Joffe, Josef. "'Bismarck' or Britain? Toward an American Grand Strategy after Bipolarity." *International Security* 19, no. 4 (Spring 1995): 94–117.

Judis, John B., and Spencer Ackerman. "The Selling of the Iraq War." *New Republic* Online, post date June 19, 2003, issue date June 30, 2003.

Judt, Tony. "The Way We Live Now." *New York Review of Books*, March 27, 2003: 6–10.

Kaiser, Karl, and others. "*Deutschland, Frankreich und Europa: Perspektiven*" ("Germany, France, and Europe: Prospects"), DGAP-Analyse 21. German Council on Foreign Relations and the French Institute of Foreign Relations (IFRI), January 2003.

Kamp, Karl-Heinz. "Prevention in US Security Strategy." *Transatlantic Internationale Politik* 4, no. 1 (Spring 2003): 1–20.

Kitfield, James. "Damage Control." *National Journal*, July 19, 2003, carried in NATO Enlargement Daily Briefing Op-Eds, July 18, 2003, distributed by the Latvian Embassy in Washington, archived at http://groups.yahoo.com/group/nedb/messages.

Kornelius, Stefan. "Joschka Fischer's Long Journey," *Transatlantic Internationale Politik* 4, no. 4 (Winter 2003).

Krauthammer, Charles. "The Unipolar Moment." *Foreign Affairs* 70, no. 1 (Winter 1990/91): 23–33.

———. "The Unipolar Moment Revisited," *The National Interest*, no. 70 (Winter 2003).

Kristol, William, and Robert Kagan. "Toward a Neo-Reaganite Foreign Policy." *Foreign Affairs* 75, no. 4 (July/August 1996): 18–32.

———. "Do What It Takes in Iraq," *Weekly Standard* (September 8, 2003) (www.ceip.org/files/Publications/2003-09-06kagan.weeklystandard.asp?from=pubdate).

Krzeminski, Adam. "Poland's Home Is Europe." *Transatlantic Internationale Politik* 4, no. 3 (Fall 2003): 65–68.

La Balme, N. "When the Going Gets Tough: Public Opinion and Transatlantic Policy Choices." Paper presented at the German Marshall Fund Pre-[U.S.-EU] Summit Symposium, June 24, 2003.

Lemann, Nicholas. "How It Came to War." *New Yorker*, March 31, 2003.

———."War on What?" *New Yorker*, September 16, 2002.

Lerman, Antony. "Sense on anti-Semitism." *Prospect*, August 2002.

Lieven, Anatol. "The Hinge to Europe: Don't Make Britain Choose between the U.S. and the E.U." Policy Brief 25. Washington: Carnegie Endowment, August 2003.

———. "Speaking Up." *Prospect* 86 (May 2003): 24–27.

———. "A Trap of Their Own Making." *London Review of Books* 25, no. 9 (May 8, 2003).

Lindley-French, Julian. "Terms of Engagement." Chaillot Paper 52. Paris: EU Institute for Security Studies, May 2002.

Livingston, Robert Gerald. "Patching Up German-American Relations." *Transatlantic Internationale Politik* 4, no. 3 (Fall 2003): 47–53.

Maull, Hanns W. "Germany and Japan: The New Civilian Powers." *Foreign Affairs* 69, no. 5 (Winter 1990/91): 91–106.

Mertes, Michael. "Anti-Americanism? Forget It!" *Transatlantic Internationale Politik* 4, no. 3 (Fall 2003), forthcoming.

Moravcsik, Andrew. "Striking a New Transatlantic Bargain." *Foreign Affairs* 82, no. 4 (July/August 2003): 74–89.

Nakash, Yitzhak. "The Shi'ites and the Future of Iraq." *Foreign Affairs* 82, no. 4 (July/August 2003): 17–26.

Naumann, Klaus. "NATO and the EU's Strategic Choices." *Transatlantic Internationale Politik* 4, no. 3 (Fall 2003): 11–16.

Nye, Joseph S., Jr. "U.S. Power and Strategy after Iraq." *Foreign Affairs* 82, no. 4 (July/August 2003): 60–73.

Occhipinti, John D. "The Impact of Enlargement on Justice and Home Affairs." Paper presented at the EUSA conference in Nashville, March 29, 2003.

O'Hanlon, Michael E. "A Flawed Masterpiece." *Foreign Affairs* 81, no. 3 (May/June 2002).

Ottoway, Marina. "Think Again: Nation-Building." *Foreign Policy*, September/October 2002, www.globalpolicy.org/nations/future/2002/0910building.htm.

Pew Research Center for the People and the Press. "America's Image Further Erodes, Europeans Want Weaker Ties," opinion survey released March 18, 2003; and *Views of a Changing World*, June 2003, http://people-press.org.

Project for the New American Century. "Rebuilding America's Defenses." Washington, September 2000, available at www.newamericancentury.org.

Quinlan, Joseph P. *Drifting Apart or Growing Together? The Primacy of the Transatlantic Economy.* Washington: Center for Transatlantic Relations, 2003.

Rabasa, Angel M. *Political Islam in Southeast Asia: Moderates, Radicals and Terrorists.* Adelphi Paper 358. London: International Institute for Strategic Studies, May 2003.

Rice, Condoleezza. "Promoting the National Interest." *Foreign Affairs* 79, no. 1 (January/February 2000): 45–62.

Risse, Thomas. "For a New Transatlantic—and European—Bargain." *Transatlantic Internationale Politik* 4, no. 3 (Fall 2003): 20–28.

Roberts, Adam. "Law and the Use of Force after Iraq." *Survival* 45, no. 2 (Summer 2003): 31–56.

Robins, Philip. "Confusion at Home, Confusion Abroad: Turkey between Copenhagen and Iraq." *International Affairs* 79, no. 3 (May 2003): 547–66.

Schake, Kori, and Klaus Becher. "How America Should Lead." *Policy Review* 114 (August/September, 2002), www.policyreview.org/AUG02/schake_print.html.

Serfaty, Simon. Testimony to the European Subcommittee of the House Committee on International Relations, June 11, 2003, wwwa.house.gov/international_relations/108/Serf0611.pdf.

Solana, Javier. "Mars and Venus Reconciled: A New Era for Transatlantic Relations." Lecture at Harvard's Kennedy School of Government, April 7, 2003, http://ue.eu.int/solana/list.asp?BID=107.

Steinbach, Udo. "The Iraqi Fata Morgana." *Transatlantic Internationale Politik* 4, no. 3 (Fall 2003): 73–78.

Steinberg, James B. "An Elective Partnership: Salvaging Transatlantic Relations." *Survival* 45, no. 2 (Summer 2003): 113–45.

———. "Re-Founding the Transatlantic Relationship." Paper presented at the German Marshall Fund Pre-[U.S.-EU] Summit Symposium, June 24, 2003, Washington, D.C.

Stephen, Chris. "Operation Anaconda." *Prospect*, December 2002.

Stern, Jessica. "The Protean Enemy." *Foreign Affairs* 82, no. 4 (July/August 2003): 27–40.

Vogel, Heinrich. "The End of the 'Old West.'" *Transatlantic Internationale Politik* 4, no. 3 (Fall 2003): 15–19.

Voigt, Karsten D. "US-EU: Putting Transatlantic Relations to the Test?" *Transatlantic Internationale Politik* 3, no. 3 (Fall 2002): 35–39.

Wagener, Martin. "Al Qaeda in Southeast Asia." *Transatlantic Internationale Politik* 4, no. 2 (Summer 2003): 85–90.

Weiler, J. H. H. "The Transformation of Europe." *Yale Law Journal* 100, no. 2 (1991): 403ff.

INDEX

ment, 69; withdrawal from NATO military command, 27, 72. *See also* Chirac, Jacques
Frankfurter Allgemeine Zeitung, 50–51, 54, 58
Friedman, Thomas, 41
Frum, David, 49
Fukuyama, Francis, 3

G-*8* summit, Evian, 83, 87
Gaddis, John Lewis, 60
Garton Ash, Timothy, 15, 43
Gedmin, Jeffrey, 38
Germany: al Qaeda members in, 9; American bases in, 57, 65, 70; American occupation, 27–28, 55; anti-Americanism, 39–40, 59; antimissile demonstrations (*1980*s), 40, 51; Bush's visits to, 57; Christian politicians, 54; commitment to nonviolence, 51–52; core European defense union, 87; democracy in, 55; disagreements with United States, 30, 56–62, 70–71, 84; election campaign (*2002*), 56, 57–61; embassy to United States, 11; environmental laws, 70; extradition of terrorists, 9; firms interested in Iraq reconstruction contracts, 81; foreign minister, 52, 61, 85, 93; foreign policy principles, 67–68; Green Party, 12, 52, 60; indirect support for Iraq war, 65; intelligence agencies, 8–9; involvement in Iraq reconstruction, 82, 86, 89; Iraq war as election issue, 57–61; navy, 53; opposition to Iraq war, 40, 51–52, 53, 57–61, 68, 70, 71, 73; postwar reconciliation with France, 14–15; postwar reconstruction, 27–28, 55; potential for nuclear weapons, 25; public opinion of United States, 10, 93; regional elections, 58; rela-

tions with eastern Europe, 68, 69, 86; relations with France, 66–68, 87, 94; relations with United States, 35, 43, 48–49, 53, 67, 70–71, 72, 93–94; role in European Union, 68; role in NATO, 25–26; support for Israel, 52; troops deployed abroad, 12, 52–53, 58, 70, 94; unification, 25, 29, 66–67. *See also* Schröder, Gerhard
Gingrich, Newt, 39, 49
Globalization, 4
Goldberg, Jonah, 41
Gorbachev, Mikhail, 29
Gordon, Philip, 5
Grant, Charles, 23–24
Grant, Linda, 41
Grass, Günter, 39
Guantanamo, prisoners held by United States, 23, 38
Gulf War, 11, 18, 45, 51–52, 55, 57, 84

Haass, Richard, 50
Habermas, Jürgen, 92
Hamas, 84
Hassner, Pierre, 13
Hirschman, Albert O., 6
Hoagland, Jim, 49
Huntington, Samuel, 31, 46
Hussein, Saddam: audio tapes of, 77; citizens killed by, 81; escape from Americans, 76; European view of, 36, 45; purported link with al Qaeda, 45, 79; relations with United States, 56, 63; support for overthrow of, 19, 20, 21, 44; survival in power after Gulf War, 18. *See also* Iraq
Hutton, Will, 22–23, 24

Ikenberry, G. John, 28–29
India, 11
Intelligence agencies: cooperation among, 8–9; evidence on Iraq's